Sea Kayakir
Florida Keys

Bruce Wachob

Pineapple Press, Inc., Sarasota, Florida

Copyright © 1997 by Bruce Wachob

All rights reserved. No part of this book may be reproduced in any form or by any means, electronic or mechanical, including photocopying, recording, or by any information storage and retrieval system, without permission in writing from the publisher.

Inquiries should be addressed to:
Pineapple Press, Inc.
P.O. Box 3899
Sarasota, Florida 34230

Library of Congress Cataloging in Publication Data

Wachob, Bruce, 1961–
        Sea kayaking in the Florida Keys / by Bruce Wachob ; foreword by Dan Tillemans. — 1st ed.
            p.   cm.
        Includes bibliographical references (p.   ) and index.
        ISBN 1-56164-142-1 (pbk. : alk. paper)
        1. Sea kayaking—Florida—Florida Keys—Guidebooks. 2. Natural history—Florida—Florida Keys—Guidebooks. 3. Florida Keys (Fla.)—Guidebooks. I. Title.
GV788.5.W33 1997
797.1'224'0975941—dc21   97-28398
                                                                                    CIP

First Edition
10 9 8 7 6 5 4 3 2

Design by Carol Tornatore
Printed and bound by Victor Graphics, Baltimore, Maryland

Table of Contents

Section III — Advanced Trips

Charts of the Florida Keys

Foreword by Dan Tillemans
Outdoor Education Director,
Cornell University

Life-giving adventure, investigation of wild ecosystems, and communication with the natural rhythms of time await the individual who is willing to travel by kayak in the Florida Keys — one of the last remaining backcountry gems for the state-bound paddler seeking a tropical coastal environment.

In *Sea Kayaking in the Florida Keys*, self-taught local expert Bruce Wachob not only provides us with the most comprehensive sea kayaking guide available (with all the inside information on the best routes, put-in/take-out points, maps, etc.), but also shares a wealth of information about the Florida Keys' fascinating natural history. Information abounds on flora and fauna from sea, land, and air.

Readable, resourceful, minimally technical, and full of information any backcountry kayaker should know, this book is indispensable for outdoor enthusiasts.

Because of this excellent field guide, the doors are now open for more people like you and me to access the one of the beautiful remaining wilderness areas on earth, hopefully to develop a deeper appreciation for the natural world. I fully support the author's intent in sharing his valuable knowledge with us, as well as his intent to encourage responsible backcountry travel. May we all leave as little sign of our passing as sunlight through air.

Enjoy this guide, and enjoy your travels in the Florida Keys.

Acknowledgments

*I*n the process of writing and editing this book, I obtained invaluable assistance from several members of the scientific and marine science community. I wish to extend thanks to George (G. P.) Schmall, Manager of the National Marine Sanctuary Program, Key West office, who worked within his special field, marine sponges, and added his thoughts on marine organisms. Also I would like to thank Lou Bulluck and Scott Wright, of the Marine Research Institute, St. Petersburg, Florida, for their help on marine fishes, marine organisms, terrestrial animals, and natural history. Jim Colvocorisses of the Department of Environmental Protection, Marine Research Branch, Marathon, Florida, offered many suggestions on crustaceans and fishes.

Special thanks to Jeanette Spindel, novice kayaker and computer instructor, who single-handedly took this manuscript from the stone age to the space age. I would like to thank my father, Harvey Wachob, for assistance with the charts that clearly show the described courses for each trip. Also, I would like to thank my employers, Tom and Elizabeth Blount of Adventure Charters and Tours, for their never-tiring patience and some last-minute photos.

Thanks to Pro Photo in Key West for their professional help in selecting the best film type and for fast turnaround of last-minute darkroom work. I would like to thank National Ocean Surveys (NOS) for their permission to reproduce their charts.

Finally, to Vieni, I give thanks for her help and patience on this important project.

Introduction

I am writing this book for those who enjoy the sport of kayaking and have a spirit of adventure. The Florida Keys have many sites for individuals or groups to explore. However, to the unfamiliar visitor, specific launch sites may seem mysterious and hard to find. This book is designed to help first-time visitors, as well as those who return every winter, familiarize themselves with the exciting world of exploring the nearshore and offshore islands and their habitats.

I grew up in the lower Florida Keys and have been a kayak guide for many years. I have watched with enthusiasm the growing interest in the backcountry islands. These are the bridgeless islands that parallel the lower Keys. Unlike other visitors who use power boats to explore the reefs and other natural resources here, the kayakers have few navigational aids at their disposal. Competition among kayak tour guides has grown fierce and a free exchange of information about where to go and where to launch is unavailable. This book is an attempt to open the door which separates the tour guides from the novices and to help visitors become more familiar with the world of kayaking the Florida Keys.

The Keys offer kayakers safe passage through one of the most biologically diverse, ecologically sound habitats in North America. Home to the only coral reef system in North America, its warm tropical waters teem with aquatic birds indigenous to this region. Whether you choose an all-day outing or only a few hours of exercise, serenity surrounds you and extends to everywhere you look as you glide quietly and gently over the shallow flats.

The tidal flats are home to a variety of birds and fish. Migratory flocks consisting of seven species of herons, three species of egrets, brown pelicans, flocks of white ibis as well as fish-feeding raptors such as bald eagles and osprey come here to share the same tidal flats with game fish, like tarpon, permit, snook, and bonefish, that attract sports fishers from around the world.

These same tidal flats share a unique relation with the offshore waters in that they are the fragile nursery that repeatedly stock the fertile fishing grounds. These tidal flats provide the food and habitat which make this area rich in the famed natural resources of the Florida Keys. Stone crab and lobster are two of the main catches of the commercial fishing industries in this area.

The kayak, with its shallow draft design and quiet maneuverability, allows you to observe firsthand the uniquely structured aquatic community without being plagued by the noise, exhaust fumes and maintenance problems of motor boating. From the kayak, our perspective of the marine habitat is different from that of other pleasure boaters. We can observe a large array of invertebrates, crustaceans, and marine sponges without putting on a mask and snorkel. However, if you love diving or snorkeling, coves, tidal creeks and patch reefs abound.

Bruce Wachob

Section 1

Description of the Florida Keys

1. Starting Out

*I*n this book, I offer the kayaker general information about the Florida Keys, including the refuge areas, the natural history, the weather and tides, and the wildlife. The information contained in this book cannot be obtained in any other single source. For your safety, I hope that you will review this portion first. I also hope that you will refer to this book often to better understand our area.

Finding your way around the Florida Keys

In spite of all the development in the Keys it is still possible to find and access areas that offer excellent kayaking experiences both along U.S. 1 and offshore in remote locations. From the Seven-Mile Bridge to Key West, there are forty miles of two-lane highways with various accessible launch sites. Beginning in Key West, the small green mile markers along the shoulder of U.S. 1 are excellent points of reference. This book will concern itself with only those markers south of mile marker 48. It is this system of markers that I will use to familiarize the reader and direct him/her to areas of interest.

The trip descriptions start with the islands south of the Seven-Mile Bridge, covering the area between mile markers 48 and 10, and there is an advanced section for those of you who are interested in a more thorough workout. The advanced island trips cover the area from approximately mile marker 25 to mile marker 6.

Sea Kayaking in the Florida Keys

In the Florida Keys, accesses to the waterways are somewhat restricted due to private ownership of some lands, but there are some choice sites which you will recognize after reading this book.

There are a number of matters to be considered when selecting a launch site. Leaving your vehicle unattended should be of concern, but, if you lock your valuables in your trunk and leave nothing in plain sight, you should be fine. Finding your remote parking site could prove difficult if you return at dusk. If you're not familiar with the area you should leave ample time for your return to avoid looking for your vehicle in the dark. Private marinas offer easy access as well as vehicle security, but they do not offer the quiet, remote surroundings most of us seek. Because they sell fuel for powerboats, as well as groceries and bait, marinas are geared for powerboating and are often located on the busy highway. Entering such areas may require caution and tolerance of the noise and traffic.

Backcountry insights

A common concern here for kayaking in the Keys is the very real possibility that at some time you may panic and feel lost. However, if you have planned your trip well in advance, you can avoid this feeling. Maneuvering the look-alike mangrove islands in the backcountry of the Florida Keys can cause the same confusion as wandering in a Northern forest. Also the looks of an area change slightly with the flux of the tides. However, because the range of your vision is much greater in open water, you have at your disposal many points of reference. Towers, channel markers, even blimps can offer good references to your position. Panic can be avoided by simply stopping and gaining your composure. Try to avoid frustration and time-consuming backtracking.

Having the right tools will help reduce confusion. As valuable as anything you will carry, a good waterproof compass

Special purpose buoys, such as this one, are found in and around the Great White Heron Refuge area. Please obey these, as well as all regulations in the Florida Keys.

can keep you from getting turned around. One common, albeit amusing, error here in the Keys is mistaking a great white heron or great egret, feeding at low tide, for a channel marker. Binoculars can help because by clearly viewing objects close to the horizon, you will make fewer mistakes in identification. Two good waterproof NOAA maps to keep on hand are Numbers 11445 and 11448. All trips covered in this book are found on these two maps and are duplicated here in part at the beginning of each trip. This is for your reference here but not for use in navigation. Please obtain your own copies of the two waterproof maps mentioned above.

Kayaking in the Keys, like sailing, is a system of self propulsion, using only your paddle, the available wind, and tidal currents to move along. Before planning a course or trip for the day, considerations of the winds and tide flow can make your trip a more pleasurable experience. By putting the most difficult leg of your passage first (upwind, against the current, etc.), you can rest assured that you will always return easily.

In the lower Keys, there are areas that have an abundance of shallow tidal basins easily accessed on windy days. I have paid considerable attention to these areas and have kayaked in these areas with great success. There is usually no reason to postpone an entire trip because of weather because there are almost always protected routes at your disposal. You should be prepared at all times for whatever the elements have to offer. This, of course, means that you should carry along plenty of water, emergency food, sun-screen with a high SPF factor, a good hat, sunglasses, extra shirts, towels, and, most important, a waterproof first-aid kit.

Going into some areas requires examining tide tables before starting out. Otherwise, you could paddle in and have to walk out, a tiring and frustrating experience. Tide information can be obtained through local bait and tackle shops and most dive shops. There are also listings for tides and some tide adjustment times in local newspapers. NOAA weather radio broadcasts 24 hours a day on Channel 5 (TCI Cable) and on Channel 2 (VHF radio weather band). Later in this book, I will explain in more detail the tidal effects on selected areas. (See section on Weather and Tides.) Navigational charts are necessary before heading out into unfamiliar waters and a review of the charts the night before can be most helpful.

Kayaking techniques

Most of the trips in this book are appropriate for the novice kayaker and do not require extensive use of kayaking techniques. When you find yourself in areas of swift current there are but a few simple rules that apply to keep you out of trouble. Consider the following whenever you work in and around tidal streams anywhere in the lower Keys.

4

- Whenever working in narrow tidal streams, always work against the tide. This will give you better control of your kayak. When working with more than one kayak, allow thirty feet or more between boats. This will keep from jamming boats together, which can cause you to unintentionally turn over your kayak.
- Paddles that can be broken down into two parts can give you more versatility in narrow areas. By taking the paddle apart, you can use one half of it like a conventional canoe paddle. A full-length paddle can be dangerous because it is awkward to use and can cause head and neck injury if it gets lodged in trees or carried off with fast-moving water.
- Approach unfamiliar turns slowly. If working downstream, let the speed of the water move you along while you use the paddle to steer and to repel trees.

An excellent general reference for choosing equipment and mastering techniques is *Sea Kayaking in Florida* by David Gluckman. See the Bibliography.

Choosing a trip

Kayaking in the Keys can be done even in the most adverse conditions. High winds can offer a challenge, but in protected areas outlined in this book, kayaking can usually be enjoyed even on windy days. With a few simple rules, consideration of everyone's skill level and carefully selected areas, kayaking can be enjoyed even on windy days in the Keys.

Round-trip distances are given in the description of each trip. In planning your trip, you may want to estimate your speed, thereby estimating travel time. The design of your kayak can affect the speed at which you can make actual time along a specific course. For the most part, conventional (sit-down-in) sea kayaks offer good performance, even in adverse conditions. Sit-upon kayaks, the most popular design for this area, though stable, can be slightly awkward in windy conditions. It is my experience that most people in generally good health can expect to make one to two miles per hour in a head wind of fifteen MPH. You can expect to make between 2000 and 3000 strokes per hour under these conditions. On the other hand, when headed downwind in the same winds, you can expect a speed of as much as five MPH, with only about 1000 to 1500 strokes per hour. Cross winds of the same velocity, on the other hand, can generally give you a forward speed of two to three MPH, with a stroke rate of 1500 to 2500 per hour.

Below I have listed all trips, classifying them by skill level:

Beginner: These trips are ideal for everyone, including novices. They can be enjoyed by everyone, even under adverse weather conditions.

1. *Bahia Honda State Park, page 78
2. *Big Pine Key (Atlantic side), page 82
4. Summerland Key, page 98
6. *Sugarloaf Key (all trips), page 112
7. Boca Chica Key, page 127

Intermediate: These trips are ideal for slightly more advanced kayakers, or for everyone on days when the weather is good.

1. Seven Mile Bridge area, page 78
2. Big Pine Key (Gulf side), page 82
3. The Torch Keys, page 93
5. Cudjoe Key (all trips), page 103

Experienced: These trips should only be done by experienced paddlers. These trips often involve hours of open water paddling, with little for shelter under windy conditions. These trips should only be done under the best weather conditions.

8. The Content Keys, page 137
9. Sawyer Key, page 143
10. The Barracuda Keys, page 149
11. The Snipe Keys, page 156

* Food and lodging nearby.

Portaging your kayak

In the unlikely event that you find yourself on the wrong side of the islands at low tide, you may consider portaging, but use extreme caution. The Keys are unique islands, largely made of sediment, and are surrounded by underwater sediment as deep as 2 feet in some areas. Finding yourself in a soft bottom area can be an unpleasant experience as well as an exhausting one. Portaging should only be attempted as a last resort. Even apparent hard bottom areas offer a challenge because the limestone is often sharp with deposits of sediment within depressions. I have found it most helpful to carry a small, thin rod for checking the amount of sediment. By pushing the rod through the soft bottom until it finds the hard "cap" rock below, you have some idea what you're about to step into. The blade of your paddle can also serve as a guide, but seldom can you push the blade more than 10 inches through the sediment.

A poling technique can be useful if the bottom is grassy and you can see somewhat deeper water close by. If you have a two-part paddle, you can pull the two sections apart and use them like ski poles. I have found this technique very helpful in muddy, shallow water. It does not work on hard bottom. Unfortunately, the bottom is seldom even, but picking and choosing your way along carefully can save you the tiresome task of portaging. Avoid high spots, such as dunes formed by sand worms and burrowing sea cucumbers commonly associated with muddy/grassy bottoms. With the wind and/or tide behind you, this task is even easier.

2. Weather and Tides

Kayaking in the Florida Keys requires careful consideration of the effects of weather and tides. The combination of these two effects can make for a pleasant experience or for a difficult passage. In this chapter, I will try to unveil the mystery surrounding these natural phenomena and try also to make sense of them for kayakers.

Tides

The Florida Keys usually have mixed tides, meaning two high tides and two low tides every 24 hours. None of these tides are of the same height. During full moon, as well as new moon periods, the effects are amplified, causing extreme highs and lows quite apparent even to the novice. These periods of higher and lower tides associated with the full moon and new moons are called "spring tides." (Note that these happen all year-round, not just in the spring.) You can usually see the effects of the spring tides some three days before and three days after the full or new moon. On the other hand, high and low tides vary less than usual at the first and last quarter of the moon. These are called neap tides. In the advanced section of this book, I describe areas where special concern should be taken around the spring-tide times of the month. To complicate things even more, winds usually associated with large weather fronts or tropical storms can further enhance the local tide effects.

There are seasonal effects that also complicate under-standing tides. The first seasonal effect starts usually in March, with a rise of about 3 inches. Then later, usually in August, the sea rises again by as much as 8 inches, peaking around late October. Then, between November and February, the sea level once again recedes until March when the cycle repeats itself. This effect is caused by the expansion of sea water as it warms in the spring and summer and the contrac-tion as it cools in autumn and winter.

The actual tide range between high and low tides is, on the average, about 2 feet. The highest tide recorded without assistance from storms is about 5 feet. The waters around the backcountry, especially around the small islands and the tidal basins that neighbor them, are seldom much deeper than the range of the tide. "The shallowness of the water in some areas can present a problem for the kayaker."

Listed here are some tide adjustments for areas around the Lower Keys. By adding or subtracting these times from Key West Harbor times, you can estimate the time for high or low tides at or near areas of interest.

Location	Time Adjustment *from Key West*	
	High tide	Low tide
Bahia Honda Key	-0.45	-0.27
No Name Key	+1.35	+1.33
Big Pine Key		
(Coupon Bight)	-0.20	+0.49
Content Keys	+2.47	+3.50
Cudjoe Key	+3.58	+3.58
Tarpon Belly	+3.07	+4.22
Sawyer Key	+2.27	+3.02
Snipe Key	+2.15	+3.33
West Harbor Key	+2.11	+3.06
Channel Key	+2.38	+2.30

Cutoe Key apprx 1 hr later than Content

Weather affecting the Florida Keys

Weather can have an adverse affect on outdoor activities such as kayaking. As with most activities, you must consider numerous factors such as time of year, time of day, local weather, and national weather effects. Fortunately, here in the islands, the weather is most often pleasant year-round for outdoor activities, but careful consideration of the weather should always be a part of your trip plan.

Cold fronts, bringing cooler weather to the Keys, occur most frequently between late November and late May. At times strong winds associated with these weather patterns offer the most challenge to the kayaker. Listening to weather broadcasts will indicate whether a day's planned activity may have to be altered or postponed.

Wind, or the lack of it, can have considerable effect on the tides themselves. The month of March can be a very difficult time for weather on the Eastern Seaboard. The Florida Keys is no exception to this rule. This is the time of year when winter and spring are struggling for supremacy. This struggle often results in high winds that last for weeks. Experienced mariners also know that this time of year is when some of the most violent storms occur. These storms always seem to coincide with the full moon in March. In recent history, the Storm of the Century in 1993 and the Blizzard of 1996 both occurred just after the full moon of March. Both of these storms brought unusually high winds and rains to our region. If you plan on visiting this area during this time of year, please plan accordingly.

Tropical weather, mostly associated with the summer and early autumn months, June through November, often spawns thundershowers. These late afternoon storms are associated with gusty winds, torrential rains, and dangerous lightning strikes. This is also the time for tropical trouble of another type — hurricanes. Fortunately, these are detected well in advance and can easily be avoided by the well-informed.

Weather and Tides

Annual rainfall in the Florida Keys is about 39 inches, with most of this occurring during the summer months, especially during the months of August and September.

3. Natural History

Thousands of visitors come annually to the Keys. Most visitors come to dive on the coral reefs. Still others try their luck fishing on shallow grassy flats for bonefish and permit or in the Gulf Stream for wahoo, king mackerel, dolphin, and marlin. Still others come just for a break in the long cold winters of the northern states. Not too often, however, do visitors look for and find something different and unique. That fortunate visitor who stumbles, either by chance or fate, upon the backcountry of the lower Florida Keys, suddenly realizes that these offshore islands are rookeries, feeding grounds, habitats, and sanctuaries to countless creatures.

It is here in the backcountry that the treasures for an entire ecosystem are kept. For without these shallow waters surrounding the myriad of small mangrove islands, the rest of the Keys would appear quite different. Without the mangroves or grassy flats, there would be no clear, pristine waters. These two plant communities trap sediments, keeping them from becoming waterborne with waves and storms. Without the mangroves and flats, silt from run-off would intrude upon the already endangered reef, causing untold damage to the coral, which needs clear, nutrient-free water to survive. As these ecosystems provide water for each other, they also provide habitat for the larger marine creatures that make the Keys such a special place.

The backcountry provides a diverse marine habitat, which is home to many aquatic birds, many species of fish and waterfowl, and a few mammals. The mangroves and shallow grass flats provide food as well as shelter for hundreds of species of invertebrates: immature lobsters, stone crabs, blue crabs, shrimp, sponge crabs, and horseshoe crabs. In the following chapters, we will talk about the important role of each species and its significance to the entire ecosystem. We will also briefly discuss the human impact on this area in the section on National Wildlife Refuge Areas.

Mangrove habitat

From almost anywhere in the Florida Keys, small dark patches of green islands grouped together in a variety of sizes and shapes dot the horizon. These are the mangrove islands, consisting mostly of **red mangrove**, *Rhizophora mangle*, so necessary to the ecology of the backcountry of the Florida Keys. The evolution of these small, sometimes submerged, islands goes back nearly one hundred thousand years to a time when the level of the world's oceans was considerably higher than today. At this time, most of what is now known as the Florida

Red mangroves like these are important to all types of bottom communities around the Florida Keys.

Keys was a reef tract. It was during this period that the limestone which is found under all the Keys was formed. The lower Keys, especially those islands south of Big Pine Key, have quite a different substratum. The pine forests and hammocks of the lower Keys occur on a geological formation known as the Miami Oolite Limestone. This limestone is composed of many small rounded particles called *ooids*. The ooids were deposited and cemented together over long periods of time when the area was submerged under a shallow sea behind an ancient reef tract. When sea levels dropped as a result of the Wisconsin Glacial Period and exposed the oolitic limestone, less resistant and softer portions dissolved, leaving a hard, pavementlike surface with many cracks and solution holes. In the lower Keys, the reefs were covered by this oolitic sand, and later, when water levels were considerably lower than today, some 100,000 years to 15,000 years ago, this oolitic sediment formed the rock we now find making up not only much of the seafloor, but the upper lands as well.

It is upon this rock that the coastal communities of the lower Keys are now based. The red mangrove traps sediment, preventing erosion and water quality problems for the reef. Other types of mangroves, including the **white mangrove**, *Laguncularia racemosa*, and the **black mangrove**, *Avicennia germinans*, are commonly found above tidal affected areas and offer little support to the marine communities. However, they play a vital role in the preservation of land areas as well as offering food and shelter for land animals.

The progression of the mangrove community is often found to be consistent with the elevation above the tide line. The red mangrove is easily identified by its stilt roots that lift it up over the water. Behind this tidal affected area, the black mangrove and the **buttonwood tree**, *Conocarpus erecta*, dominate where tide exposure is limited to only a few times a year. Black mangrove is easily identified by dark, scaly bark with salt-encrusted leaves. Also a common characteristic are the

A mature black mangrove displays its pneumatophores
toward the receding tide water.

The propagules of the
red mangrove mature
during the summer
months.

aerial roots, or pneumatophores, that poke up all around the base of the trees. White mangroves, the least common of the mangroves, are found usually behind the black mangroves in the progression shoreward. White mangroves commonly occur in the tidal creeks sporadically growing with the red mangroves. Identified by a white scaly bark and oval leaves, they display an almost waxy appearance.

Worldwide, there are over fifty species of mangroves, all of which are salt tolerant. The seeds of these mangroves are different from those of land plants because, when they fall from the parent plant, they are actually miniature replicas of the adult. These unique seeds are called propagules. They can be found on any of the mangroves here in the Keys, but those of the red mangrove are the most obvious. Long, green, and slender in appearance, with a reddish-brown pointed bottom, they often hang in clusters on the adult trees most of the summer and fall. After falling into the water, they can float and seed themselves with other colonies or support the colony from which they fell. They can float a very long ways, even across the ocean, to seed on a new shore. Those which do not take root or float away can often be found along the debris line of seashores here in the Keys.

Since 1985, mangroves have been protected from disruptive practices, such as dredging, filling, and clearing, by the Mangrove Protection Act and have been placed on the list of special concern. Because they are the predominant shoreline vegetation in the Keys, they help us to maintain a healthy coastal environment and serve as an ally against shore erosion.

Nearshore communities

Directly offshore of any island in the Florida Keys can be found the communities that are so important to all forms of life in the Keys. These are the shallow, often grassy, flats and shoals buffering the deeper reefs and channels that neighbor the Florida Keys. In and around these flats and shoals can be found a diversity of organisms that blend into a harmony of existence so critical to the welfare of all related onshore and offshore communities that they are often either overlooked or completely ignored by most visitors. It is these communities that make kayaking in the Keys different from kayaking anywhere else in the world. These shallow waters, if observed carefully, will reveal their secrets to those who watch and listen. In this chapter, I will help the observer to discover and appreciate this part of our unique ecosystem.

Nearshore communities are divided into two classifications, depending on the type of bottom. They are "hard bottom communities" and "seagrass or soft bottom communities." First, we will discuss the significance of the hard bottom communities.

Hard bottom communities

The hard bottom communities are those areas that have very little sediment upon the hard, rocky bottom. It is in this area that the marine sponges, soft corals, and some hard corals are found. They also harbor a wide variety of crustaceans (crabs, shrimp, lobster) in all phases of development, as well as many species of echinoderms (starfish, sea urchins, and sea cucumbers). Many species of fish, sting rays, and sharks can be found around these habitats. Because the bottom is light in color, due mostly from sediment or sand, it reflects light. Thus, you can recognize hard bottom communities by their light color in shallow water.

Hard bottom identifies predominantly the areas which have less than an inch of sediment on the underlying limestone rock. On the Atlantic side of the Keys, it occurs from the shoreline out to depths of about 16 feet. Florida Bay and the Gulf of Mexico have a mixture of grass beds and hard bottom in shallow water.

Solution holes are pits common to limestone rock. Rain water can accumulate in these holes. Over thousands of years, erosion has formed pits of irregular shapes. Now, fish and lobster use these holes as hiding places in hard bottom communities. Whenever portaging your kayak, be sure to wear reef slippers and beware of these depressions in hard bottom areas.

Seagrass communities (soft bottom)

Seagrass communities are arranged in much the same fashion as hard bottom communities except that they have the accumulation of more sediment, which allows the development of sea grasses. Under the shallow water, these prairies of largely **turtle grass**, *Thalasia testudinum*, allow for quite a different habitat, one usually for young, if not almost embryonic-size fish, crustaceans, and mollusks. These shallow, grassy plains, along with the coastal red mangrove areas, provide everything that young, developing fish need for their

Sea grasses, like these turtle grasses, provide a healthy habitat for developing sea life of all kinds.

first few months of existence. Countless marine organisms call these soft bottom areas home. These prairies very often are ravaged by power boats that thoughtlessly scar them with their props, as the recreational boaters or commercial fishers take advantage of this fertile habitat. It is easy to see the evidence, even from a kayak. White blazing trails that go off in any direction show up very well against the darker sea grasses. I doubt very seriously that there is a single square mile anywhere in the Keys that does not have this ugly mark somewhere within it.

It should be apparent by now that each component in this delicate ecosystem plays an important role in the stability of our environmental community, for without the benefits and support of each element in this equation, this wonder of nature could be lost. Only now are we beginning to understand the impact of human encroachment in these communities.

Scenic mangrove communities which have endured a millennium of storm abuse overhang tidal-fed waters.

4. Marine Organisms

Marine organisms are too numerous to count. We will discuss the more common varieties of species that are found in the Florida Keys, especially those which you are most likely to encounter while kayaking. Unfortunately for our visitors, there are fewer and fewer species to observe in the great numbers that once flourished here. The taking of fish and crustaceans for food and the capture of live specimens for aquariums have had an increasingly adverse effect on an already stressed habitat.

Other than the obvious marine animals, such as fish, there exist many "lesser" organisms of tremendous importance to both the habitat and the food chain. Below is a brief description of most marine organisms, beginning with the lower forms, that you will encounter in nearshore waters around the Florida Keys. I have learned that using a small dip net to capture these small marine animals is helpful in observing them up close. When we are observing crabs and other invertebrates, or any other marine animals, we treat them delicately and return them unharmed.

Marine sponges

One could very well devote an entire lifetime to the study of marine sponges. Certainly they are numerous enough in the tropics. Marine sponges are unique organisms that represent a deadend in the evolution of animals. That is to say, no

Loggerhead sponges, found commonly on hard shallow bottoms, can often resemble man-made intrusions.

higher organism ever evolved from the sponges. These animals have their own sub-kingdom within the animal kingdom. Their phylum is Porifera, which means porous animal. These simply structured animals feed entirely on plankton and bacteria which they filter from the water. Unlike living coral, marine sponges are hearty animals and can tolerate being touched. However, because of their skeletal structure, often composed of spicules of silica, touching them can leave you with an itching, burning sensation. There are well over a hundred species of marine sponges throughout the Caribbean, and most of these can be found here in the Florida Keys, usually in and around hard bottom communities and the reef. The most common varieties that a kayaker might encounter while traveling are the larger species of sponges. These are the **loggerhead sponges**, *Spheciospongia vesparium*. They are characterized by a tirelike appearance with a white hard exterior and a black porous center. These sponges are not uncommon in sizes up to 3 feet across. They provide refuge for juvenile lobster, snapping shrimp, and fish. Another common variety of marine sponges is the **vase sponge**, *Ircinia campana*. This sponge is characterized by a dark brown bowl-shape on its underside. Beachcombers collect vases to use as hanging planters, but live vases should not be disturbed. **Bleeding sponge**, *Oligoceras hemorrhages*, gives out a red liquid when squeezed. The ridges of the black and gray **cake sponge**, *Ircinia strobilina*, make it easily identifiable. The **stinker sponge**, *Ircinia felix*, forms in bunches of brown to yellowish nodes or lobes and gives off a strong, unpleasant odor. Some less common varieties are the **chicken liver sponge**, *Chondrilla nucula*, and the **tube sponge**, *Callyspongia vaginalis*.

The **fire sponge**, *Tedania ignis*, orange in color and causing burns when it comes into contact with the skin, can attach itself on hard bottom or to the dangling root systems of the red mangrove. The fire sponge is one of most prevalent sponges in tidal creek areas. Be careful not to touch or come in contact with these sponges. They can give the affected area a burning sensation that can last for hours, and because the spicules get embedded in the skin, there is no first-aid for the sting other than the passing of time.

Sponging, as an industry, is still done right here in the Florida Keys. There are several species of marine sponges here in the Florida Keys that are suitable for commercial harvesting, though only two species, the **lamb's wool sponge**, *Hippospongia lachne*, and the **yellow sponge**, *Spongia barbra*, make up the bulk of the commercial harvest. When they are alive, they look much like black or deep purple orbs on the hard bottom. Sponges are harvested by using a sponge hook, a claw-looking device attached to a long pole. After harvesting, they are dried in a shady place on the sponging boat. Then they are placed in net bags on the stern of the boat and submerged in water for a few more days. About a week after first harvesting, they are taken from the water, given a light thrashing with a wooden paddle, and are readied for market.

The taking of commercial sponges by diving or snorkeling is prohibited in the Florida Keys.

In addition to the commercial value of marine sponges, these animals play an important role in the commerce of our islands in a unique and indirect way. The very existence of a healthy sponge community means the existence of a healthy crustacean community: the crabs, shrimp, and lobster that have been harvested commercially for nearly a century in this part of the world. Sponges provide habitat and a source of food for young crustaceans of all kinds, especially juvenile spiny lobsters. If we lose our marine sponges, we could very well see a great decline in the fishing industry as a whole.

In recent years, the Everglades National Park area of Florida Bay has had severe sponge die-offs corresponding with the occurrence of major algae blooms which have dominated the bay. Blame is actively passed around. Some blame the Florida Water Management District's periodic decision to release fresh water into the bay. FWMD controls central and south Florida's water flow through a system of canals and culverts. Water management practices since the early part of this century have changed the natural water delivery schedule to the Everglades and Florida Bay. Some experts feel that every time flood control is exercised, the release of nutrient-rich water into Florida Bay fuels recurrent algae blooms, causing sponge die-offs.

Although the Keys are far removed from agriculture, which is responsible for the high nutrient content of the run-off, we must keep a close eye on the Everglades and Florida Bay to ensure our lasting economy. In early 1994, scientists from the Nature Conservancy, the Florida Marine Research Institute, and Florida International University began collecting water-borne samples from high-chlorophyll areas. They are hoping to record, over time, the salinity of the water and the densities of suspended carbonates or phytoplankton concentrations, which in some areas are one hundred times normal.

The ecology of the Everglades affects the Keys in that the natural flow of water from Florida Bay passes to the Keys via Lignum Vitae Key and through Long Key Channel Bridge. The entire ecosystem, including the living coral reef, is at risk.

Cnidaria (jellyfish, sea anemones, and coral)

This section looks briefly at the marine organisms that are by far the most biodiverse in our waters. Not only do these creatures make up the hard corals that are commonly found around our reef, but they also include the soft, jellylike animals. Different members are parts of both the nearshore and offshore communities.

Jellyfish

In this group of marine organisms, the kayaker will probably encounter only one. It is found in areas where the muddy bottom is exposed and an accumulation of sediment kills the growth of the turtle grasses. This jellyfish, *Cassiopeia xamachana*, the **upside-down jellyfish** or the **mangrove upside-down jellyfish**, can accumulate in numbers that nearly blanket the exposed sediment. These slightly toxic jellyfish are about 3 inches in diameter but can be much larger. The generally mild sting from these jellyfish can easily be relieved with cortizone cream or spray. Unlike its ocean dwelling cousin, the **moon jellyfish**, it lies on the bottom with its smooth side down. The animal exposes its underside toward the sun where its tentacles absorb the cultures of symbiotic algae which it eats. The presence of this algae can cause these animals to appear almost light green, but they can appear brown or even golden yellow. Not only are they present in backcountry lagoons that do not often get tidal currents but they also are found carpeting most Keys canals as a sign of oxygen-depleted, nitrogen-rich waters.

Sea anemones

Sea anemones represent a revolution in evolution. They bridge an important gap between true jellyfish and hard corals. With their bases firmly planted on the bottom and their often colorful tentacles displayed upwards, they can appear as flowers in the gardens of Neptune. In the shallow waters surrounding the Florida Keys, the most common variety is the **pink-tipped anemone**, *Condylactis gigantea*. Found around shallow grass beds, this animal is about 3 inches across and displays white or pink tentacles. If you were to touch the animal, you would find that it has an almost adhesive quality, which enables it to trap its small prey.

Hard corals

Though most true hard corals are in deep water, there are a few types that are hearty enough to survive even the shallowest of marine environments. Though these species don't form reefs, they still represent an important part of the ecosystem, and, like all true corals, are very fragile animals. It is important to know that the taking of coral, living or dead, is illegal.

One of the more common species of corals found in tidal areas, associated with hard bottoms, is the **golf ball coral**, *Favia fragum*, which looks much like the name implies. Almost as common is the **lesser starlet coral**, *Siderastrea radians*. These small brown corals are no larger than 3 inches across and can be found anywhere that hard bottom is present. Another type of coral that is commonly found in shallow, hard bottoms is **thin finger coral**, *Porites furcata*. The small but densely placed "fingers" of this animal form small clusters, often spreading for acres. Finger coral can appear brown or tan and has also been found in an unusual purple variety in the lower Keys. This type of coral is very important to the development of smaller crustaceans and other invertebrates. Often you can find small brittle stars (starfish) among clusters of this coral.

The **rose coral**, *Manicina areolata*, is found in a little deeper water than the previous species but usually in no more than 12 feet. Appearing much like brain coral, this tiny, grooved coral seldom reaches 4 inches in length. It dwells primarily on sandy bottoms where tidal flow is predominant. One of the more amazing features of this coral is that it sits in sand on a pedestal of about 1 inch, not attached to hard bottom.

Echinoderms (starfish, sea urchins, sea cucumbers)

Echinoderms, or spiny-skinned animals, are of the next class of marine organisms. These include starfish, sea urchins, and sea cucumbers. Most of these simple sea creatures are found throughout the different types of marine communities and at various depths.

Starfish

Worldwide there are over one thousand species of starfish. They can be divided further into two classes: **sea stars**,

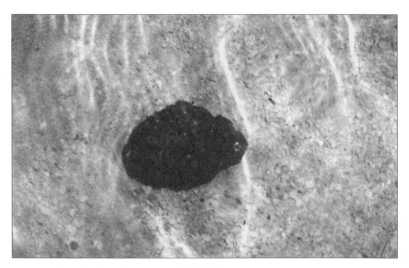

Rose coral can be found on sandy tidal-fed bottoms in water as shallow as a few inches.

Asteroidea, and **brittle** or **serpent starfish**, *Ophiuroidea*. We will concern ourselves with only a few of these species. The most common variety of sea stars is the **thorny sea star**, *Echinaster sentus*. It is dark brown to tan in color, with tiny thorns on the top exterior, and seldom exceeds 6 inches across. This sea star is commonly found throughout the shallow waters of the Florida Keys.

The **cushion star**, *Oreaster reticulatus*, is certainly the most beautiful and impressive of all the starfish in this part of the Caribbean. Other common names are **Bahama star** and **reticulated star**. It grows to more than a foot across and is bright orange in color, making it easy to spot while you are kayaking or snorkeling. Because of their size and beauty, cushion stars have been harvested to near extinction. Harvesting or possessing a cushion star in state or federal waters is prohibited. Penalties include a fine up to $600 and a misdemeanor charge.

This Bahama star (also known as cushion star), is an endangered species. Fines of up to $600 are levied on those who illegally harvest them.

The sea egg can be found in very shallow waters around hard bottom communities.

Sea urchins

These animals are by far the best representatives of their phylum for they truly are spiny-skinned. Here again there are many species throughout the world, but only a few common varieties are found locally.

The **long-spined black urchins**, *Diadema antillarum*, which are more frequent around reefs, are the most familiar sea urchins. This species in particular now exists only in very limited numbers due to a virus in the late 1980s that nearly wiped them from the reefs. Harvesting or possessing a long-spined sea urchin in state or federal waters is a misdemeanor with fines up to $200.

More commonly found on the deeper grassy flats and around tidal creeks are the **variegated urchin**, *Lytechinus variegatus*; the **sea egg**, *Tripneustes ventricosus*; and the **red heart urchin**, *Meoma ventricosa*. These species display short spines with rounded ends and are harmless to handle. They are most commonly found covered in debris such as sea grasses, shells, and leaves, making them hard to detect.

Sea cucumbers

The sea cucumber is by far the most common member of the Echinoderms found in nearshore waters. This simple creature reminds us of a slug. At least a dozen varieties are found locally. However, nearshore varieties are restricted to only one common species, the **Florida sea cucumber**, *Holothuria floridana*. It can be up to about 10 inches in length. It is often covered in the sediment in which it is found. It has an almost black-looking skin when it wishes to display it, but it prefers to remain covered in silt most of the time. Equipped with a "walking sole," it moves about eating the sediment and extracting anything organic, including bacteria, from it. When removed from the water, the sea cucumber can squirt water from its anus. Sea cucumbers are usually found in large groups; seldom is only one found at a time.

Arthropoda (crabs and lobsters)

Actually, this section is about Crustaceans, one of the more important food sources for the higher marine animals. All of these species have segmented bodies and hard outer shells and are nocturnal by nature. Though there are several species that have adapted to living out of water for long periods of time, we will cover only one in particular in this section, the land hermit crab.

Crabs

These diverse animals are most abundant in all types of habitats. They come in all sizes, shapes, and colors, with their own roles to play in nature.

The swimming crabs, crabs with flat, paddle-shaped hind legs, are actually quite abundant in our waters. One in particular, the **blue crab**, *Callinectes sapidus*, is often found near the red mangrove, foraging in the soft muddy sediment. If approached or disturbed, it will burrow very quickly into the fine sediment. Swimming crabs are largely nocturnal, feeding

A giant hermit crab, shown here occupying a horse conch shell, needs a larger shell than its smaller cousin, the green-striped hermit crab.

under the cover of darkness when they are less vulnerable to predators.

Another common crab found throughout tropical waters uses sea shells from dead sea snails for a temporary dwelling. The **green-striped hermit crab**, Clibanarius vittatus, is commonly found in the shells of the true tulip or other light, small shells. These crabs have a land-dwelling cousin, the **land hermit crab**, Coenobita lypeatus, found around the Keys in hardwood hammocks. The taking of these land creatures as pets to sell to tourists has greatly depleted their numbers. The green-striped hermit crab can usually be found in shallow tide pools and near the mangroves as well. I have seen them grouped in numbers of about fifty at a time. They often appear dark green, with yellow or white vertical stripes running the length of their legs. Another species, though not as common, is the **giant hermit crab**, Petrochirus diogenes. Usually found living in large shells, like that of the queen conch, these crabs are red and very rough-looking creatures. Please respect these animals. They do not forfeit their shells easily, and without killing the animal, there is no way to separate the crab from the shell.

One of the strangest crabs is the **common spider crab**, *Libinia emarginata*. This small crab, usually no more than 2 inches across, can be found in shallow tidal areas, lying on top of the turtle grass. It is often white and slow-moving. You can easily handle one because its claws offer little resistance. This animal often covers its outer shell with living grasses and sponges to blend into the natural habitat.

Another backcountry inhabitant, the **arrow crab**, *Stenorhynchus seticornis*, is dainty. Not more than .5 inch wide and 2.5 inches long, it is pale gray, cream-colored, buff, or orange with inverted, v-shaped, light and dark brown or black stripes with a solid arrowhead-shaped body. One of the more unusual of the backcountry crabs, it is delicate and must be handled with care.

The next species of crustacean is a culinary variety, the **stone crab**, *Menippe mercenaria*. Commonly harvested in the Florida Keys, this crab has very powerful claws. When harvested, only the claws are taken, and the animal is returned to the sea where it will grow a new claw, making it one of the few replenishable food sources of its kind. It is one of our great delicacies. Recreational harvesting of stone crab claws is permitted in season (October 15 through May 15), but there are restrictions on the taking. See your local bait shop or call the Florida Marine Patrol (305-289-2320) for specifics. The crab can be found along hard bottoms especially where sponges are common. Stone crabs blend in well with the bottom, but if you look carefully, you can see where the animal has cleared rubble away from its burrow, leaving the bottom a grayish color. Though sluggish in movement, this animal requires a careful approach. Its pinch is strong enough to break skin; even the young in the species can draw blood!

Sea Kayaking in the Florida Keys

Of all the crabs, two are more predominant than all the others. These are the **wharf crab**, *Sesarma cinereume*, and the **marsh crab**, *Sesarma reticulatum*. These crabs, though abundant, can be very difficult to see. When first encountered, they are often mistaken for spiders. At low tides, they can be found close to the water's edge, dangling from the prop roots of the red mangrove or above the water's edge along the bottom of white mangrove trees. These small crabs, usually no longer than an inch, can move very quickly and often shuffle out of sight around the root or tree trunk. The wharf crab is certainly more abundant than the marsh crab though they are almost indistinguishable.

Probably the strangest and oldest living crab is really not a crab at all. The **horseshoe crab**, *Limulus polyphemus*, is a distant cousin of the land-dwelling spider. It is the oldest living arthropod and has survived some three hundred million years in this current phase of evolution. This strange and unusual creature can be found anywhere along the shallow bottom

The molted shells of the horseshoe crabs are commonly found throughout the Florida Keys.

communities, though most commonly in muddy or grassy bottoms. The females can reach a size of 12 inches across; the males are about half this size. Either can reach lengths up to 2 feet. They are often found in an unusual mating ritual where the male attaches itself to the larger female, who tows him around. When a suitable place is found for laying eggs, the female lays the eggs, and the male simply fertilizes them. There is no intercourse in this courtship.

Lobsters

Another popular edible crustacean is the **crawfish,** or **West Indies spiny lobster**, *Panulirus argus*. These animals, unlike their northern ancestors, have no claws but have a spiny carapace. They swim backwards very fast to elude predators in and around nearshore waters. In their younger phase, crawfish serve as an important food source for other marine inhabitants of the mangrove islands and Florida Bay. Crawfish, like many crustaceans, live in and around sponges and in hard bottom areas. Often, all you will see are the "whips" or antennas of these creatures protruding from shallow sponges or rocky crevices.

One of the biggest attractions of the Florida Keys in late July is the crawfish miniseason. During the two-day event, divers in Monroe County are allowed to take six lobsters each day. No night diving is allowed in the Keys, and trapping is prohibited. This two-day hunt is probably responsible for more coral wreckage than any other single phenomenon. In recent years, the management of John Pennekamp State Park in Key Largo has recommended to the Florida State Marine Fisheries Commission that lobster harvesting be prohibited in the park because tourist divers too often damage the reef as they probe the coral for the spiny delicacies. It is of great concern to the admirer of the tropical fish and the reef system that this two-day event not inflict damage that could last for centuries.

Please follow the rules for participating in crawfish season. Get a saltwater fishing license with a crawfish stamp. Take only crawfish that are greater than 3 inches in carapace length from the eyes to the end of the carapace. Measure them in the water. If the crawfish has any red eggs attached to its underside, leave it alone. Spearing is not allowed nor is trapping or the taking of molten (soft) lobster. Open season for commercial divers is early August. Licenses for commercial divers specify different limits than those designated by the crawfish stamp used for the sport divers. For more information concerning lobster season rules and regulations, please contact local dive shops, marinas, or the Florida Marine Patrol office (1-800-DIAL FMP).

Somewhat smaller and darker than its common cousin, the West Indies spiny lobster, and a frequent visitor to our reefs, the **Spanish lobster**, *Panulirus guttatus*, or **spotted lobste**r is dark green in color with white spots. It is not common near shore nor in Florida Bay waters, is mainly found on offshore reefs.

Oddest-looking of the lobster family, looking like a blunt shoe, the **slipper** is rare, but not impossible to find on patch reefs and offshore. There are no size or bag limits for this variety. The brownish shell is very coarse. As with all lobsters, be sure to check the underside of the animal for female "feathers." If fertilized eggs are present (a dark spot will be noticeable on the belly), please return to the sea to ensure next year's crop.

Mollusks (shellfish)

Seashells of any variety, when displayed, show the beautiful exoskeleton of a once-thriving marine organism. Many shells, covering a living organism, are not easily found because the animal lives below the sediment that accumulates in and around these islands, and because these sea creatures have a clever way of covering their attractive outer shells. Mollusks, like many animals, have natural predators from which they must constantly hide. Some cover their backs with algae and sponges, while others cover themselves with mud or other sediments. Some shellfish display a natural coloring that simulates their natural surroundings.

In the Florida Keys there is no commercial industry concerned with the taking of mollusks. In years past, however, there was a sizable industry in the harvesting of queen conchs. Today, there is a fine of up to $500 for the possession of one. They are being raised in captivity on Long Key and reintroduced into the environment in the hopes of bringing them back from near extinction. The Marine Research Institute, a branch of the Department of Environmental Protection, has been funded by the United States Department of Commerce for this study. It has been ongoing since 1987 and has had only partial success.

Most species of mollusks discussed here can be found either in the Atlantic or the Gulf of Mexico. However, some are found exclusively on one side of the islands or the other. If your interest is in shell gathering, locate shells that have been vacated by their inhabitants. The process of removing these animals for the purpose of preserving the shell is not an easy one and requires time and know-how. If the animal is not removed entirely, the shell will always emit a foul odor. You should never attempt to remove the animal from a live shell.

Shellfish can further be divided into two groups. Those like clams and scallops are called bivalves because their shells have two distinct halves. Univalves, like the queen conch, have a single shell.

Common bivalves

Bivalves such as clams and scallops occur near shore, mostly around the Gulf side of the islands, in sandy bottom where storms and tides cover and uncover them with shifting sand. The most common of these is the **tiger lucina**, *Codakia orbicularis*, with an almost perfectly round shell that is all white with a woven texture. Other types include the **speckled tellin**, *Tellina lister*, and **sunrise tellin**, *Tellina radiata*. Shells of these varieties are nearly oval in shape and display patterns that coincide with their names. Other commonly found bivalves include the **turkey wing**, *Arca zebra*, which slightly resembles an oyster in shape, and the large, frail **amber penshell**, *Pinna carnea*, which when seen in the water resembles a beautiful peach-colored, elongated fan standing up on end in the sand. It is seen in sizes to 6 inches and found in depths up to 50 feet.

Common univalves

Listed below are a few common species of univalves. Keep in mind that they are difficult to distinguish in their natural habitat.

Queen conch — This astonishing mollusk is found only on the Atlantic side of the islands and is most commonly located on grassy or sandy flats. Its shell can reach a length of 9 inches and has a flared lip when matured. It has a golden skin on its outer shell, which is usually covered with sediment. The underside of the shell displays a range of colors from creamy pink to vibrant chartreuse. It is found at depths from 3 to 100 feet.

Other conchs — The **milk conch**, *Strombus costatus*, a smaller, yet thicker cousin of the queen conch, is often found on the Gulf side of the islands. The milk conch displays a light brown back and a white underside, suggesting its name. The shell is about 5 inches in length, when the conch is fully grown, and displays the flared lip that all adult conchs have. They are very amorphous and the underside of the shell itself is white. They occur commonly in tidal streams and on shallow rocky bottoms.

Another small conch that is not nearly as common is the **fighting conch**, Strombus alatus. This animal's shell is seldom larger than 3 inches in length at maturity. Like all of the others mentioned, this conch shell has the flared lip when the conch is mature. It displays brilliant colors of orange and dark brown. Fighting conchs are most commonly found on shallow sandbars associated with those islands closest to the Gulf of Mexico. They get their common name from their habit of struggling to free themselves from the hands of unwary would-be collectors.

Whelks — There are two common types of whelks that can be found in the lower Keys, mostly on the Gulf side of the islands. The **lightning whelk**, Busycon contrarium, is the largest and most commonly encountered in the Florida Keys. It can reach 10 inches in length. Smaller members of the species are more brilliantly colored, with brown bands, than the larger adults which are mostly white. The shell itself is long and tapered except where the shoulders form a club at the end. Along the top of the shoulders, a row of knobby points projects outward from the shell. Lightning whelks live mostly on sandy bottom where they feed primarily on scallops and clams. During the winter months, they are commonly found near shore where they breed and lay eggs. These are spiral pods, often 2 feet in length, usually attached to the bottom. Their eggs can be often seen along shallow sandbars in the winter.

Another common species, though not as large, is the **pear whelk**, Busycon spiratum. The shell of this smaller cousin of the lightning whelk is also smoother in texture, lacking the knobby points along its shoulders. It seldom reaches more than 3 inches in length. This species is marked with a white background and brown bands.

Tulips — Tulip shells are among the most common variety of mollusks found in the Keys and are almost always inhabited by a hermit crab after the original animal has died. The

Lightning whelks like these are common along sandbars in the Florida Keys.

shells are commonly found on rocky bottoms in shallow waters. These animals are the most aggressive mollusks. They feed on nearly all other types of mollusks, including each other.

The **true tulip**, *Fasciolaria tulip*, is the most commonly encountered. The shell can be described as a smooth spiral, tapering from the shoulders to a fine point. In the Keys, they are usually black or dark brown with white highlights. If the shell is held out of the water for a short period, the animal will display itself. It is dark brown or black with tiny white spots throughout. The mature size is about 9 inches, though smaller specimens are more common.

The **horse conch**, *Pleuroploca gigantea*, is not a conch at all but rather a large tulip. This shell is one of the largest in the world. A childhood associate of mine once found one measuring 20.5 inches. Though not the largest specimen ever found, it was certainly a remarkable find. The horse conch has a rougher texture than the common tulips but still has the same basic design. The live animal is a brilliant orange and is commonly found on and around grassy, sandy bottoms. They eat a wide variety of other mollusks, including the queen conch. They are found in the Atlantic as well as in the Gulf.

Other common univalves — Other commonly found mollusks include the **Caribbean vase shell**, *Vasum muricatum*, which occurs often in areas where true tulips are found. This animal covers itself very cleverly with algae and sediment to hide from the tulip shell. Often, the only way to find this master of disguise is to follow a wide trail in the sand to what appears to be a rock. If you pick the animal up, it will reveal its white underside. This animal is seldom larger than 3 inches in length.

Another common univalve that dwells near shore, usually in muddy, still waters, is the **king's crown**, *Melongena corona*. Somewhat smaller than the vase shell, this animal covers itself with whatever is available. It can be found by following the trail its shell leaves in muddy sediment where it forages for food.

Human impact on mollusks

Conch shells are among the most sought after by collectors. Their beautiful array of colors and shapes are most pleasing to the eyes. For this reason alone, the numbers of these univalves have diminished the world over. The Florida Keys are no exception. Commercial fishing traps, used to trap lobster and stone crab, are also appealing to these types of mollusks. Once caught, they are usually taken because they provide the fisherman with another source of income, selling them to collectors or to wholesale dealers. Today, a number of these once-common species are considered endangered. Through major efforts, these animals could have a chance to return to their once-flourishing numbers here in Florida.

By far the most popular among local people, the shell of

the queen conch has graced the Monroe County seal for over one hundred years, leading to the name the "Conch Republic." The people that settled this area before the turn of the century were called "Conchs" (pronounced "konks") because before refrigeration these once abundant univalves served as an important food source for indigenous people. The meat was dried and cured, then eaten later. The meat of the queen conch, *Strombus gigas*, can still be purchased in many forms (chowders, fritters) but it is acquired from other Caribbean nations such as the Bahamas, Turks, Caicos, and the Cayman Islands. Queen conchs have been protected in the waters of the Keys since 1985 because of overharvesting. Harvesting or possessing a queen conch in state or federal waters is a misdemeanor with fines up to $500.

Queen conchs are important to the shallow grass areas because they eat harmful algae that can plague these fertile grasslands. They are commonly encountered in Bahia Honda

The queen conch is an emblem of the people who settled the Florida Keys.

State Park, where they have been reintroduced by the Florida Marine Research Institute. The Keys Marine Lab on Long Key, headed by research scientist Bob Glazer, has been carefully hand-raising the tiny mollusks for reintroduction. The program was the result of the persistence of former Keys State Representative Joe Allen more than ten years ago. As of late 1993, as many as 900 had been placed oceanside in the Middle Keys.

The nearshore water quality in the upper Keys has taken its toll on the hatchery on Long Key. It is being directly affected by the flow of water from Florida Bay. The sea water at the Long Key facility on the gulf side of the Keys is "biologically rich" and "contaminating" to the baby conchs. Despite budget cuts faced by the Marine Fisheries Commission, resident managers of this project hope to be able to continue to monitor stocks and complete the rehabilitation of the queen conch throughout the lower and middle Keys.

5. Nearshore Fishes

*T*his chapter discusses the more common species of fish that will be encountered while kayaking around the Florida Keys. The species of fish encountered in shallow areas are quite different from those inhabiting offshore reefs. Most of the fish that you will find are not brightly colored and, therefore, are more difficult to see, especially to the untrained eye. You should give yourself a little time to become accustomed to the fact that most fish in the nearshore community look much like the surrounding habitat. It is even more of a challenge to locate fish on cloudy days or during the early morning and late afternoon.

These fish are divided into two general categories: those with cartilaginous skeletons and those with bony skeletons.

Cartilaginous fish

Sharks, as well as skates and rays, are cartilaginous fish having no true bones. They do have a backbone, but even this is made of cartilage. The cartilaginous fish are predominant in nearshore waters. This does not mean that the nearshore waters are, by any stretch of the imagination, shark-infested or that there are hungry man-eaters about. Quite to the contrary, most of the sharks that you will encounter are not only small but are easily frightened, even by kayaks. In general, there are only four cartilaginous fish commonly encountered while kayaking in the Florida Keys.

Stingrays, often large and always powerful, make for an anxious moment when startled.

Found in water as shallow as a few inches or as deep as 40 feet, the **Southern stingray**, *Dasyatis americana*, is a graceful, but powerful, animal. These rays can grow to more than 3 feet from wing tip to wing tip. While kayaking, look for disturbed areas where the soft, muddy bottom has been churned up, making the water appear cloudy. This is often a sure sign that a ray is working the bottom for food. As large as these animals are, they can be very swift and stealthy in shallow water.

The **nurse shark**, *Ginglymostoma cirratum*, of the carpet shark family, appears somewhat lazy. It is unique because it can lie on the bottom and still manage to breathe. It is often found basking on the bottom, appearing to be asleep. With its tan to brown coloring, it can blend into a grassy shallow bottom and remain unnoticed. Usually nurse sharks encountered in shallow waters are only a few feet in length whereas larger individuals (up to 14 feet) are found in deeper waters.

Lemon sharks, with their near perfect color scheme for
nearshore waters, can go by unnoticed.

The **bonnethead shark**, Sphyrna tiburo, is a small member
of the hammerhead shark family. It is common in nearshore
waters when temperatures are cooler. This shark is remarkably
fast and easily frightened. It is called "bonnethead" because
of the peculiarly shaped head, much like that of a round-blad-
ed shovel. It seldom exceeds a length of 40 inches.

The **lemon shark**, Negaprion brevirostris, is by far the most
exciting animal to find and probably also the most difficult to
see. In and around the shallow basins of the Florida Keys,
smaller lemon sharks are abundant. I have, however, encountered individuals in excess of 7 feet, in just a few inches of
water in areas around Cudjoe Key. Their gray coloring gives
them almost a shadowy appearance, even when viewed closely. With their black-tipped fins, they are often mistakenly
called "black tips." None of these sharks, if left alone, poses
any threat to the kayaker.

Nurse sharks are a common site along the Florida Keys.

Bony fish

This section includes all of the other non–game fish species, beginning with the smallest, that you are likely to encounter while kayaking in the lower Keys.

Silversides, the tiny wonders of the nearshore waters, are found abundantly around mangrove islands. Usually found massed in small schools, they serve as an important source of food for many juvenile game fish. When disturbed by a small predator, the silversides are often seen springing from the water in great numbers. They glisten like diamonds as they make their airborne escape from predators. Two types of silversides are commonly found here in the Florida Keys: the **hardheaded silverside**, *Atherinomorus stipes*, a species found almost exclusively in the lower Keys; and the **Keys silverside**, *Menidia conchorum*, which is now on the endangered species list.

45

Pinfish, Lagodon rhomboides, flourish in and around grassy bottoms. They are often captured in small wire traps and sold live to game fisherman. They can often go unnoticed because of their coloring, which blends well on grassy bottom.

Needlefish are very common throughout the Keys. In nearshore waters, these slender fish appear very near the surface and are barely detectable. They have a light green dorsal surface with silver sides which make them almost invisible. The most common of the family is the **redfin needlefish**, Strongylura notata. This species can reach 2 feet in length. When startled, they leap from the water and "walk" nearly upright on their tails across the surface of the water.

The small **yellowfin mojarra**, up to about 9 inches in length, is very common near shore. The yellowfin mojarra, Gerres cinereus, is found only in small schools. This broad, silvery fish with a forked tail of gray vertical stripes is very difficult to see because of its natural camouflage.

Mullet are by far the most plentiful of all the fish in the nearshore community. In the winter months, they can appear to dominate the shallow muddy basins in and around the lower Keys, especially in the Sugarloaf Key Sound areas. The **white mullet**, Mugil curema, is elongated with silvery sides and a dark dorsal surface. It has a large head but a very small mouth, looking much like a small torpedo. It seldom exceeds 1 foot in length near shore. The other more common species, **liza**, Mugil liza, is smaller still and is found throughout South Florida and the Keys. To locate mullet, look for areas of muddy water. When they feed, they stir up bottom sediment, causing a large cloudy area in the nearshore waters. If you kayak through this area, they might jump out of the water. It is also very common to see pelicans in the waters where the mullet are feeding, as well as osprey in the air above. These fish are commonly found in bait shops in Florida and are edible, generally being served fried or in spreads. These fish were caught in large numbers using large nets until a state law was passed banning commercial net fishing in all of the state waters.

The **gray snapper** is one of several species of snappers, found commonly around the shallow islands and near the mangroves, especially in their juvenile stages. Commonly called the **mangrove snapper**, *Lutjanus griseus*, because of its close association with mangroves, this fish is found offshore as well. It has a large mouth with well developed teeth and a dark stripe on the head. It grows up to 3 feet in length but seldom reaches this size in nearshore waters.

Next to sharks, probably the most feared fish in our tropical waters, and the most misunderstood, is the **great barracuda**, *Sphyraena barracuda*. Very small barracuda can be observed around mangrove islands. Long and silvery, they have a most impressive display of teeth and a healthy curiosity. It has been said, repeatedly, that they are attracted by shiny objects in the water, like jewelry. There is probably no denying this; however, if left alone, they are not likely to attack.

Nearshore game fish

Though a few of the previously mentioned fish can be placed in this category, the ones mentioned below support an entire industry throughout the Keys. Guides in specially designed crafts stand on elevated platforms to search out these fish. Pushing the shallow draft skiff quietly over calm flats with a long pole, the guide can spot these very elusive fish and direct anglers where to throw their bait.

From the seated position in your kayak, it is most difficult to spot these "ghosts" even under the best of conditions. In case you are lucky enough to spot one or more of these elusive creatures, I have described them here. Nearly all of these species are caught and released.

By all means, the **tarpon** is one of largest of the nearshore game fish in the Keys. This large silvery fish can sometimes reach 5 feet or more in length and weigh more than 100 pounds. Tarpon, *Megalops atlanticus*, often seek out their prey in small schools. They are often observed playing much like porpoises, rolling their backs out of the water and even waving their tails.

The rarely seen **bonefish** is by far the most elusive fish of the nearshore waters. Nicknamed the "gray ghost," the bonefish, *Albula vulpes*, is the prize fish of most trophy hunters. It is a very strong fish for its size (seldom larger than 10 pounds).

A relatively common member of the jack family, the **yellow jack**, *Caranx bartholomaei*, is found in the nearshore waters during the winter months. Yellow jacks are often found in small schools. They average about 10 pounds. I have often seen them accompanying large lemon sharks in and around nearshore waters.

A member of the jack family, the **permit** grows to be about 40 pounds in size. The permit, *Trachinotus falcatus*, is considered a delicacy by sport and spear fishers. In my opinion, the permit is probably the most stunning of the jack family to observe. The wide silvery body and long dorsal and anal fins make the fish look much like a diamond.

More commonly found in the upper and middle Keys, **snook** are one of the larger game fish, often weighing up to 40 pounds. They are found in tidal creeks and in the shade of mangrove islands. Once common around the bridges, the **common snook**, *Centropomus undecimalis*, was nearly fished out of existence because of its favorable size and delicious flavor. Today they are protected by size restriction and a closed season.

6. Aquatic Birds

Aquatic birds are the species of birds that feed primarily on fish or other marine life. Here in the Florida Keys, since this form of food is the most abundant, these species are the primary residents. These marvels of nature can be categorized by both the type of prey they seek and the methods they use to capture prey. There are many publications specializing in just our local species. By no means are the species listed here the only ones to be found. A more complete list of the 285 species which can be found in the Keys throughout the year can be acquired from the Key Deer Wildlife Refuge headquarters in the Winn-Dixie shopping plaza on Big Pine Key or from any of the Monroe County libraries. This list is provided courtesy of The Florida Keys National Wildlife Refuges. The book *Florida's Birds* by Kale and Maehr (see Bibliography) is also recommended.

Wading birds

These birds are the species most commonly seen while kayaking. The order, *Ciconiiformes*, includes the herons, egrets, ibis, and spoonbills.

Herons are commonly found around shallow, grassy flats during the low tide. It is interesting to note that the **great blue heron**, *Ardea herodias*, which is typically blue-gray, is found in the Keys in two other color phases not commonly found anywhere else in North America. A white color phase,

The great white heron, the namesake of its own refuge, is a common sight in the Florida Keys.

or "morph," was once considered a separate species and called a great white heron. It can be distinguished from the great egret by its very large size (50 inches instead of the egret's 40 inches). The other unusual color phase is actually a "hybrid" with a dark body and white head and neck.

Although most of these wading birds may be found together feeding on the same flats during low tide, the types and methods of catch vary. Nearly all herons seek their prey by "still hunting," a technique in which the bird stands in shallow water (or on a low branch in smaller species such as the **green-backed heron**,) and waits for fish to happen by.

Though great blue herons are found throughout the Keys year-round, they are seen more frequently during the months between November and April. The night herons, such as the **yellow-crowned night heron**, *Nyctanassa violacea*, and the **black-crowned night heron**, *Nycticorax nycticorax*, are usually seen only during the midwinter months. They return to the northern Florida during the summer. The green-backed heron,

Butorides striatus, on the other hand, is found most commonly during the summer months. These short-legged herons are cleverly colored to match perfectly in red mangrove habitat. It has been my observation that these tiny herons will not even show up on a two-dimensional image, such as a photograph, unless there is a neutral background. The tiniest heron, the **least bittern**, *Ixobrychus exilis,* is even more elusive than the green-backed heron.

Three species of egrets are commonly found in the Florida Keys: the great egret, the reddish egret, and the snowy egret. Egrets, like herons, are tall birds with long legs that they use for wading and fishing. The distinction between egrets and herons is not always easy. While the **great egret**, *Casmerodius albus,* always has black legs, the great herons tend to have lightly colored, usually orange legs. The **reddish egret**, *Egretta rufescens,* can be found in the Florida Keys with plumage in either the red/gray phase or the white phase. This can often lead to confusion with other species of heron, namely the **lit-**

A yellow-crowned night heron is easily flushed from its mangrove roost.

This reddish egret, rusty in color, is distinguished from
other egrets by its two-toned bill.

tle blue heron, Egretta caerulea, which, when adult, is almost a
deep slate blue. While in the juvenile phase, the tricolored
heron, Egretta tricolor, is about the same size as the little blue
heron but is more brightly colored. The reddish egret has a
two-toned beak, lightly colored toward the face and black-
tipped. This bird has a unique way of feeding. By spreading its
wings out and chasing fish, it herds them into a school, then
plucks them out. This technique is called "canopy feeding,"
and the reddish egret is the only species of bird that feeds in
this manner in South Florida.

The snowy egret, Egretta thula, is a small, dainty, white bird
which, like most egrets, is found during the midwinter
months. Snowies are often seen in small flocks and are easily recognized by their outstanding legs and feet. Their legs are
black with bright yellow feet, giving them the look of having
"little golden slippers." Like other herons and egrets, in the
spring they wear their beautiful, feathery breeding plumage.

Other wading birds, such as the **white ibis**, *Eudocimus albus*, enjoy a diet of crustaceans and insects. White ibises are seen mostly working muddy flats where the tidal waters have receded to expose small crabs and shrimp. Their curved beaks are well suited for the task of probing and recovering these small morsels. These white birds with black wing tips are found most abundantly during the midwinter months. White ibises nest in large colonies of fifty or more. In recent years, the ibis population in Florida has fallen more than 60 percent and in 1994 the bird was listed by the state as a "species of special concern." Except for the wood stork, none of Florida's other wading birds are on the threatened or endangered list. It is thought that reduced numbers are due to shrinking habitat and loss of wetlands due to construction and agriculture.

The last wading bird that we will discuss is the **roseate spoonbill**, *Ajaia ajaja*. This pink-tinted bird is certainly a sight to behold with its pink wings and back, orange tail, bright red rump and long, flattened bill. The light pink of immature birds gradually deepens to bright pink in the adults. Although spoonbills nest in large colonies in Florida Bay, I have spotted several in the Big Pine Key area and Lower Sugarloaf Sound. They are also frequently seen west of the county beach on Boca Chica Key, at the end of Boca Chica Road directly behind the Naval Air Station.

Diving birds

These large fish-eating birds of the order *Pelicaniformes* have short legs and large wings.

Brown pelicans, *Pelecanus occidentalis*, are a common sight throughout Florida in general, and the Florida Keys are no exception. These large, cumbersome birds can be seen in small flocks, often in formation. They search the surface waters looking for schools of fish, then dive upon their prey from unbelievable heights. Landing head first, they capture their prey with ~~their long beaks.~~ in their throat pouches

wrong!

53

Sea Kayaking in the Florida Keys

The **double-crested cormorant**, *Phalacrocorax auritus*, is by far the most abundant aquatic bird in the Florida Keys. Cormorants form large flocks and colonies around isolated mangrove islands in and around the backcountry. They are jet black with orange hooked beaks and webbed feet. They can dive to great depths, reportedly as great as 70 feet, to capture their prey in their beaks, but are very poor fliers. They are found in the Keys year-round.

The **magnificent frigate bird**, *Fregata magnificens*, is the most awesome flier of all the aquatic birds. Not truly diving birds, these birds scavenge or steal from other birds. Their large wing span (7.5 feet), unique wing form, and deep-forked tail give them an ominous appearance. The males are solid black except for a red throat pouch. Females have a white breast patch. These birds are found in the Florida Keys mostly in the midwinter months and whenever a storm pushes them back from the deeper regions of the Caribbean. Although they are found in limited numbers year-round, they are making a comeback because of recent endeavors to protect nesting sites. Part of the National Marine Sanctuaries Plan is to prohibit water craft in nesting areas.

Raptors (birds of prey)

These shy birds are the most magnificent and by far the most sought after by birding enthusiasts. Only two common species of the order *Falconiformes* are found in and around our marine habitat. **Ospreys**, *Pandion haliaetus*, are by far the most beautiful found here. They often nest in the winter months, using the same site each year. More mature adults commonly lay two-egg clutches in January. Come spring, the pairs leave their young for one season while they go north to other regions to lay more eggs and raise a second batch of offspring. Frequently, their nests are found on telephone poles. They also are very reclusive and have low nesting sights in and around all the offshore islands. This can make kayaking into these regions really special. Be sure not to flush them ~osprey~ from their nests during their egg-laying period (from January to March approximately). If the female is flushed for longer than 10 to 15 minutes, the egg can die. Such a threat makes no-wake zones and designated protected areas here a real necessity.

A few other species of raptors are found here on occasion. The **bald eagle**, *Haliaeetus leucocephalus*, a threatened species, nests here in the Keys in limited numbers. It can be seen if you are really vigilant. Much more commonly seen is the osprey. Also called a fish hawk, it is often seen plunging into the water feet first to catch a fish, which it then takes to a tree to eat. Sightings of the threatened **peregrine falcon**, *Falco peregrinus*, the largest falcon found in Florida, are uncommon in the Keys. Look for the distinctive eye/cheek patch that extends over its head,

Turkey vultures, *Cathartes aura*, are common in the Florida Keys, making their return to the area as cold weather in the winter months makes the search for food more difficult up north. This bird of prey, though not very attractive with its bare red head and its penchant for eating carrion, fills a rather important niche in the cycle of life in the Florida Keys. Turkey vultures are often found circling overhead in large flocks around larger islands of the Florida Keys. They glide ever so effortlessly on warm air currents associated with the larger islands.

Shorebirds

One would not expect this type of bird to fare well in the Florida Keys, since the mangroves make up most of the coastal region and there is little, if any, real shoreline. These birds are found in limited numbers throughout the Keys and have adapted means of support. Their order, *Charadriiformes*, includes gulls, like the **laughing gull**, *Larus atricilla*, and the **ring-billed gull**, *Lairs delawarensis*; and terns, such as the **royal**

Shorebirds like these dowitchers can appear suddenly out of mangroves in remote areas accessible only by kayak.

Shorebirds like this whimbrel are not common in the Keys year-round.

tern, *Sterna maxima*, and the **least tern**, *Sterna antillarum*, which is on the threatened species list but is trying to make a comeback. (Once again, loss of habitat is cited as its nemesis.) Sandpipers and plovers, members of *Charadriiformes* known for their chattering colonies, include the **short-billed dowitcher**, *Limnodromus*; **ruddy turnstones**, *Arenaria interpres*; and occassionally the **whimbrel**, *Numenius phaeopus*.

Rookeries

There are areas that seem for one reason or another to attract more birds than others. These areas, called rookeries, are frequented year after year by the same species. Nearly all the aforementioned birds are found in and around these areas, with the exceptions of raptors and shorebirds.

Large numbers of cormorants, pelicans, egrets, herons, and frigate birds nest in dozens of small offshore mangrove islands. When you are kayaking, these islands are easy to spot because their upper regions are white-specked with the guano of the birds. Approach slowly and they will remain for close examination and interesting photos.

One well-known and easily kayaked rookery is the island directly offshore of Blimp Road in the Cudjoe Key trip section. You can see nearly all the aquatic birds nesting at this sight. Sunset is the best viewing time. Whenever possible, I have included rookeries in the site-specific trip descriptions.

Wildlife rescue

There are a few organizations in the Keys that will respond to an emergency call concerning any wildlife. One is the Wildlife Rescue League (294-1441). If you find any wild bird that has been injured, perhaps having been hit by a car or tangled in monofilament fishing line near bridges or anywhere on the water, they can hospitalize the animal and do emergency medical treatment. The birds are cared for on-site at

*This majestic mangrove island overhanging tidal waters
is an offshore rookery and nesting site for herons,
egrets, and cormorants.*

Sonny McCoy Indigenous Park. The organization operates
solely on donations. On several occasions I have seen cormorants that were unable to feed as a result of some acci-
dent. If you see an injured bird, put a piece of cloth or towel
over it until it can be picked up. Covering it has a calming
effect on the bird and keeps you from being bitten. The
Wildlife Rescue League will usually come at any time, day or
night, from Key West to the middle Keys.

7. Mammals and Reptiles

Marine mammals
There are only few varieties of marine mammals that are indigenous to these tropical waters. The most common encounter is with the **Atlantic bottlenose dolphin**, *Tursiops truncatus*. These marine mammals are often seen in nearshore waters year-round. They are seen individually or in large pods, numbering ten or more. They are always a pleasant sight and are generally playful. It has become increasingly popular to swim with dolphins because of their gentle

Atlantic bottlenose dolphins play along the coasts of the Florida Keys.

nature and the safety of our waters, though we do not recommend you try it without expert supervision.

Another marine mammal of the Florida Keys is the sea cow, or manatee. Sea cows migrate through the Keys during the fall months on their way to their winter destination, the Crystal River. The big, plant-eating **West Indian manatee**, *Trichechus manatus*, is one of the most gentle creatures among the marine mammals of South Florida.

The water surrounding the Florida Keys are too shallow to support larger marine mammals such as whales. **Humpback whales**, *Megaptera novaengliae*, do migrate around the Florida Straits and into the Gulf of Mexico in the winter months, but they seldom come closer than 20 miles from the shore. The **short-finned pilot whale**, *Globicephala macrorhyncha*, is a smaller whale common in the north Atlantic and has been seen around the Keys, sometimes within a mile of the shore. There have also been beachings of these whales as recently as 1995 in the Big Pine Key area. Sightings are most common in the mid-summer months.

Sea turtles

Sea turtles are found all over the world in warm, subtropical waters. In years past, Atlantic green turtles, now endangered, were harvested in the Caribbean and brought to Key West for market. This practice continued until 1971 when the industry ended. Today, even possessing any part of a sea turtle is illegal in the United States. The largest threats to sea turtles today are pollution and development along coastal beaches where sea turtles have nested for millions of years.

Here in the Florida Keys, the most common species are the **Atlantic hawksbill turtle**, *Eretmochelys imbrecata peninsularis*, and the **loggerhead turtle**, *Caretta caretta caretta*. Other possible species you might encounter include the **Atlantic green turtle**, *Chelonis mydas mydas*; the **leatherback turtle**,

Dermochelys coriacea coriacea, the most rare of all sea turtles; and the **Kemp's ridley turtle**, *Lepidochelys kempi*, also known as Atlantic ridley turtle. Four of these species are endangered; only the loggerhead is considered threatened.

Nesting occurs from March through June throughout the Caribbean islands and the Florida coast. Common nesting sites in the Keys occur in the Key West National Wildlife Refuge, Great White Heron National Wildlife Refuge, and the Key Deer National Wildlife Refuge. It is rare to come upon a nesting site, but if you should, do not disturb the eggs or allow dogs near the site.

Land mammals

Land mammals in the Florida Keys are found primarily on higher ground associated with hardwood hammocks. Thus, you are not very likely to see many while kayaking. There are many species of land-dwelling mammals, with Big Pine Key having the most potential for offering a view of animals mentioned in this chapter. Nearly all of these animals have a mainland predecessor. Researchers believe that Keys mammals, after years of isolation and evolution, have adapted certain characteristic features, making them slightly different from their mainland counterparts. Many species of mammals in the Florida Keys are considered separate species, found only in the Keys. Mentioned here are some of the more common ones.

Key deer

These small, endangered deer are similar to the white-tailed deer found throughout Florida and much of the eastern United States. The **Key deer**, *Odocoileus virginianus*, were nearly hunted to extinction by 1950, when there were fewer than fifty. They were placed on the endangered species list in 1967. Today they number about three hundred and are constantly at

Key deer, though endangered, are not camera shy, and are a common sight at Watson's Hammock on Big Pine Key.

The Keys raccoon is found throughout the Keys. It feeds on blue crab, sea grapes, and anything it can forage.

the center of controversy on Big Pine Key, where their main threats are the automobile and housing development.

Raccoon

These scruffy creatures are found throughout the Florida Keys. The **Keys raccoon**, Procyon lotor auspicatus, like the Key deer are somewhat smaller and have a lighter color than those found in the rest of Florida. While kayaking, I have seen them most often around rocky areas during low tide close to the mangroves, where they forage for crabs and fish.

Lower Keys marsh rabbit

Little is really known about the endangered **lower Keys marsh rabbit**, Sylilagus palustris paludicola. With very little remaining habitat in the lower Keys, marsh rabbits make their homes mainly on the island of Boca Chica, although they have been seen as recently as 1995 in the Lower Sugarloaf Key area where there are small plots of undisturbed wild grasses. Loss of habitat is the main reason for their demise. The most striking feature about this creature is the size of its ears, scarcely bigger than an adult's little finger.

Reptiles

Most reptiles are not very fond of the salt water that surrounds the Florida Keys. There are areas where sufficient fresh water will support a small population. For this reason you will probably not encounter any of these animals while you are kayaking.

American alligator

These reptiles are common to all of South Florida, including the Everglades, but are only occasionally sighted in the Florida Keys. This is due largely to the alligator's need for fresh water. They are likely to inhabit any naturally occurring cenote (sinkhole, land depression) where fresh water collects. The most common place to find the **American alligator**, *Alligator mississippensis*, is on Big Pine Key at the "Blue Hole" (see chapter on Big Pine Key). I have never actually seen them while I was kayaking here in the lower Keys, but this does not mean you will not. During mating season in early summer, they are a common site in canals and ditches on Big Pine Key and No Name Key.

American crocodile

Unlike its close cousin, the American alligator, the **American crocodile** can live exclusively in salt water. American crocodiles are found almost entirely in the upper Keys near the Everglades National Park in a protected bay called Crocodile Lake National Wildlife Refuge. Posted as no-entry zones, bays and sounds in that region are set aside for their protection from poachers. Poachers can make large sums of money on the black market in alligator and crocodile hides. The American crocodile, *Crocodylus acutus*, is not considered dangerous and is seldom reported in the lower Keys. It is still on the endangered species list. Of the fewer than six hundred individuals, only approximately fifty of these are breeding adults.

Turtles (freshwater)

There are but two distinct types of these found in the Florida Keys. The first is the **Florida box turtle**, *Terrapene carolina bauri*, which is found around the highlands of the Florida Keys in general. This species seems consistent with its counterpart throughout Florida.

The **Key mud turtle**, or **mud walker**, *Kinosternon bauri bauri*, is rare. Found only on a few of the islands of the lower Keys, it is somewhat smaller than those found elsewhere in Florida. These turtles are found near areas where fresh water is abundant year-round, such as cenotes (limestone depressions). During times of drought they hibernate in the mud and wait for the rainy season, June through October.

Snakes

Nearly all species of snakes found in the Florida Keys have a counterpart in the eastern United States. None of these will be encountered while kayaking with the exception of the **mangrove water snake**, Nerodia fasciata compressicauda, a threatened species, also known as the **Florida ribbon snake**. It is harmless and very rare, as well as difficult to spot among the roots of the red mangroves. I have seen it on fewer than ten occasions in over a thousand trips. To evade possible predators, it drops its head to the bottom of the shallow water, allowing its body to rise and sway with the tide, imitating a fallen branch or mangrove propagule.

The mangrove water snake, though not uncommon, is difficult to find in its natural habitat.

Other common species found in the Keys — all nonpoisonous — include the **Southern black racer**, *Coluber constrictor priapus*; the threatened **Eastern indigo snake**, *Drymarchon corais couperil*; and the **corn snake**, *Elaphe guttata rosacea*. The only true recognized venomous snake in the lower Keys is the **Eastern diamondback rattlesnake**, *Crotalus adamanteus*, found in hardwood hammock areas such as Watson's Hammock in Big Pine Key.

Other species include the **Big Pine Key ringneck snake**, *Diadophis punctatus acricus*, a threatened species; the **red** or **rosy rat snake**, *Elaphe guttata rosacea*, a species of concern; and the threatened **Florida brown snake**, *Storeria dekayi victa*. Though you shouldn't expect to encounter any of these snakes while kayaking, they are mentioned here to inform you of the general Keys wildlife population.

8. National Wildlife Refuge Areas

The lower Keys offer some of the most remote areas of all the Keys. Often there are miles of open water between places of interest; camping may not be allowed in some of these remote places. This should be considered if you wish to pass several days at a time enjoying the sport of kayaking. Four wildlife refuge areas can be found in the Florida Keys. In fact, nearly all the lower Keys fall into a wildlife management area of one type or another. The Great White Heron National Wildlife Refuge and The Key Deer National Wildlife Refuge occupy nearly all the lower Keys and even overlap each other. The Key West National Wildlife Refuge occupies those islands west of Key West to the Marquesas Keys. Crocodile Lake National Wildlife Refuge will not be covered in this book because it resides more within the boundaries of the Everglades National Park. Still, the area covered by these refuges includes over 23,000 acres of land and 349,000 acres of open water.

In 1990, Congressional legislation created the National Marine Sanctuary, including all the Florida Keys and parts of the Everglades National Park, and provided a federal management plan, which has been in the works since 1992. The management plan provides for no-wake zones and no-entry zones — clearly mapped out for visitor and fisherman alike. The purpose of the new plan is the re-establishment of a balance in the ecosystem of this section of the country, a means to save marine and land animals from endangerment and extinction. Within this area we have twenty-two federally listed threatened or endangered wildlife species.

Great White Heron National Wildlife Refuge

The Great White Heron National Wildlife Refuge is an aquatic preserve including a vast array of pristine, isolated Keys, and covering over 264 square miles of open water in the Gulf of Mexico. Established in 1938, it offers protection and preservation areas for the largest of North America's wading birds — the great white heron. It is made up largely of small shallow flats and tidal creeks and is a unique location for kayaking, offering challenging open water as well as calm, clear tidal creeks for viewing marine life and birds.

This refuge covers about 7,500 acres in backcountry islands and extends to the headwaters of the Gulf of Mexico. Rare birds, such as the roseate spoonbill and the only known

Great White Heron Refuge offers open water as well as flats and tidal creeks.

colony of laughing gulls, are found nesting here in the refuge area. The boundary of the Great White Heron NWR extends from just north of Pigeon Key, off the Seven-mile Bridge, to north of Flemming Key off Key West. Diving and fishing are permitted activities in this area as long as you abide by the rules and regulations. (Please contact any bait and tackle shop or dive shop for a list of sizes and bag limits on common species of fish.) Personal watercraft, such as jet skis, Sea-Doos or Wave Runners, are prohibited in this area. This fact alone is inviting to the kayaker because there is less competition for space. Several places are "vessel exclusion" areas that are marked by the refugee management office and are discussed in the Advanced Trips section of this book.

Key Deer National Wildlife Refuge

The Key Deer National Wildlife Refuge was established in 1957 out of concern for conserving a herd of fewer than fifty deer. It is an area of critical concern for the lower Keys because it is home to the endangered Key deer, of which there are only about three hundred at present. Approximately twenty-two species on the endangered, threatened or "species of concern" lists live in this wildlife refuge. Below is a table which lists these creatures and their status.

Also the refuge is home to a variety of unique West Indian plants, songbirds, and scorpions. Centered around the island

American alligator	threatened
Atlantic green turtle	endangered
Atlantic hawksbill turtle	endangered
Atlantic ridley turtle	endangered
bald eagle	threatened
Big Pine Key ringneck snake	threatened
brown pelican	species of concern
Florida brown snake	threatened

Florida ribbon snake	threatened
indigo snake	threatened
Key deer	endangered
Key mud turtle	endangered
Keys silverside	endangered
least tern	threatened
leatherback turtle	endangered
loggerhead turtle	threatened
lower Keys marsh rabbit	endangered
osprey	species of concern
peregrine falcon	threatened
piping plover	threatened
red rat snake	species of concern
silver rice rat	endangered
Southeast snowy plover	threatened
West Indian manatee	endangered
white crown pigeon	threatened

Endangered — indicates the species is in danger of extinction throughout all or a significant portion of its range.

Threatened — indicates the species is likely to become an endangered species within the foreseeable future throughout all or a significant portion of its range.

Species of concern — indicates that the species may become threatened if not protected and effectively managed.

of Big Pine Key, the refuge covers approximately 240 square miles made up of 8,009 acres of land and the surrounding bays. It consists mainly of tracts of dense mangrove, pine rockland, hardwood hammocks, and freshwater wetlands. Nearly half of its area is shared by the Great White Heron National Wildlife Refuge. One significant difference in the regulations of this area is that the area *not* shared by the Great White Heron can be used by personal watercraft operators.

There are areas set aside for hiking, but signs that read "Do Not Enter" should be obeyed. Strict law enforcement curbs traffic within the town limits of Big Pine Key to a daytime speed of 45 MPH and a nighttime speed of 35 MPH. The speed limit within the park itself is 30 MPH. There is a simple reason for this: The Key deer are exactly the same color as the surrounding vegetation, making them very difficult for motorists to see.

Key West National Wildlife Refuge

This refuge was the first national wildlife refuge to be established in the Florida Keys. It encompasses over 375 square miles of open water and 2,019 acres of land. The Key West National Wildlife Refuge is a unique area because it is composed of islands west of Key West that protect habitat for a wide variety of birds, including nesting and wintering populations of frigatebirds, ospreys, and great white herons. The sandy beaches are nesting sites for the endangered Atlantic green and loggerhead sea turtles. The refuge was established by Theodore Roosevelt in 1908 to curtail the slaughter of egrets, whose feathers were highly valued in the production of hats and other articles of clothing. The waters between Key West and the refuge are known for sudden weather developments and tricky reefs and shoals. This area offers little protection from the elements but can offer a look into the old world of the Keys. Miles of open water surround the few islands in this refuge area, so be sure to have a plan before venturing out.

Crocodile Lake National Wildlife Refuge

Located in the Upper Keys, Crocodile Lake National Wildlife Refuge is closed to public access to protect the critical habitat of the endangered American crocodile, Key Largo wood rat, Key Largo cotton mouse, and other wildlife. Studies are conducted in this area by state-sponsored personnel to keep track of the population and to report on poaching.

Section II

Description of Nearshore Trips

Introduction

 In this section, I have outlined trips in selected nearshore areas of the Florida Keys that are good for kayaking. The selections have been made to give the kayaker the widest variety of the most interesting and remote sites. These trips can be made by everyone, regardless of age or skill level, provided the weather conditions are favorable.

I have included charts to familiarize you with the areas. Please use the charts provided here for familiarizing yourself with the general area and as references for the trip descriptions. Public put-in sites are described for each trip and marked on the charts. Please access the water only through public lands.

Using the charts

In each chapter that follows, I've included charts, or maps, to guide you. These pages are reproductions from National Oceans Survey charts and are not intended for navigational use.

On the next page are the legends for each chart included in the following chapters.

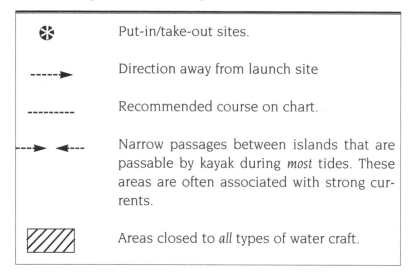

❊	Put-in/take-out sites.
-----▶	Direction away from launch site
---------	Recommended course on chart.
---▶ ◀---	Narrow passages between islands that are passable by kayak during *most* tides. These areas are often associated with strong currents.
▨	Areas closed to *all* types of water craft.

There is no prescribed way to follow the course of each trip. However, you should plan each trip before setting out. Take into consideration the skill level of all members of your party, the difficulty of the course, how long you want to be out on the water, and the conditions of the weather, winds, and tides. Remember to always plan to do the most difficult leg of your trip first to ensure safe and easy return.

A long-sleeved shirt, hat, sunglasses, and a healthy application of sunscreen on all exposed skin complete a kayaker's wardrobe for a full day of adventure.

1. Seven-Mile Bridge to Bahia Honda State Park

This chapter will cover those areas of interest around the gateway of our wonderful lower Florida Keys. We start with the small island of Little Duck Key found just after mile marker 48. **Veterans Park**, a small, sandy park on the Atlantic side, and a **boat ramp** on the Gulf side of the highway are ideal for **launching (site 1-A)**. Either side puts you in at the Seven-mile Bridge and offers easy access to small islands to the east. Molasses Key and the Money Keys are excellent islands to explore. The farthest, just over two miles from the launch site, is Molasses Key on the Atlantic side. This area is ideal for both beginners and experienced kayakers and offers a look at the diversity between the Gulf and Atlantic waters. Sandy bottoms with soft corals are found in abundance on the Atlantic side, and shallow grass flats are the ruling feature on the Gulf side. Caution should always be used around all bridges. Tidal currents and power boats can make conditions hazardous, especially for diving.

Our next point of interest is **Bahia Honda State Park**. Like all state parks, there is a visitor's fee. **Kayaks are available for rent** by the hour or by the day. Kayaking is permitted only in the areas outside the swimming areas, so **launch areas (site 1-B)** are restricted. However, there is still plenty of room for kayaking. One of the best parks in the state, nestled nicely in the southeast corner of the National Key Deer Refuge,

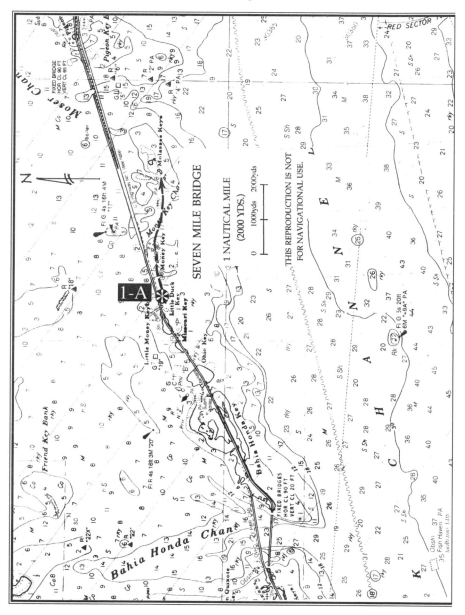

Seven-Mile Bridge

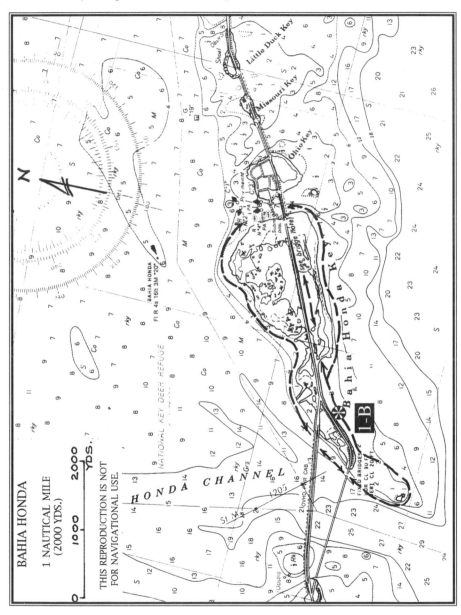

Bahia Honda

Beautiful tropical scenes like this one at Bahia Honda Key make kayaking in the
Florida Keys unlike anywhere else in North America.

Bahia Honda has a natural sand beach on the Atlantic side of the park, one of the most beautiful beaches in Florida. *Conde Nast Traveler* listed this as the "Best Beach" in America in 1992.

On the west side of the park, a deep channel passes under a unique steel bridge, built as part of Henry Flagler's railroad project. The deep channel for which this island was named spills into the Straits of Florida, giving it one of the most exciting backdrops anywhere. Diving from your kayak, you can explore endless wonders of a small patch reef near shore. In the southwest corner of the park, there is a small rock and sand island just offshore, excellent for making a brief stop on your way around the park. There is a unique tidal passage that opens the interior of the island on the Atlantic side where many species of aquatic birds and small fish can be discovered.

Camping accommodations are available. However, sites are usually full during the peak season (the winter months).

Since these two sites are largely open water, the inexperienced kayaker should exercise extreme caution during windy conditions. In the summer months, this area is excellent because of its openness and the cooler Atlantic waters.

2. Big Pine Key

(Including Coupon Bight and Newfound Harbor on the Atlantic side and Annette Key and Cuttoe Key on the Gulf side)

Located in the heart of the Key Deer National Wildlife Refuge is the largest island of the lower Keys, Big Pine Key. Leaving Bahia Honda, traveling south on U.S. 1, you soon see signs warning about the endangered key deer. Please obey these signs and drive "deerfensively." These animals are indigenous to only a few of the lower Keys. They are smaller than their mainland predecessors and have evolved with the ability to swim, which allows them to survive in the harsh environment of the lower Keys. By swimming from island to island, they can take advantage of the fresh water supplies on remote islands, then return to their main habitat, Big Pine Key, when those water supplies are depleted. I have witnessed the deer swimming only twice in my thirty years of living in the lower Keys, but you might get lucky if you are watchful and conditions are right. Most crossings are at twilight hours.

Located on Big Pine Key at the Winn Dixie Shopping Plaza is the **Wildlife Refuge Headquarters**. Turn right (south) at the light at the intersection of Wilder Road and Key Deer Boulevard and drive one block. The office is located in the south wing of the plaza across from the public library. Any questions you may have concerning this or any of the wildlife refuges in the lower Keys can be answered at this office.

Big Pine Key is a vast island with probably the most potential in all the lower Keys for kayaking. Because of its size, we

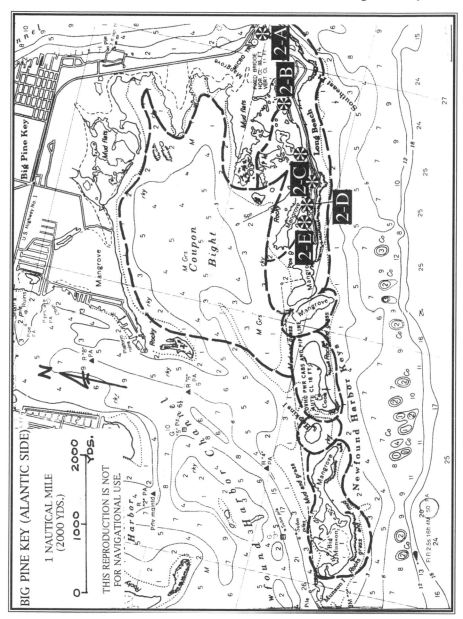

Big Pine Key (Atlantic Side)

will view it in two sections: the south side of the island on the Atlantic, where Newfound Harbor and Coupon Bight are found, and the Gulf side, where small scattered islands abound.

Atlantic side of Big Pine Key

Entering Big Pine Key from U.S. 1 southbound, you pass over Spanish Harbor Bridge and by mile marker 33. On your left is a resort lodge called Big Pine Key Fishing Lodge (305-872-2351). **Efficiencies may be rented** or **camping accommodations are available for tents and RVs.** There are two **launch ramps (site 2-A)**, fish cleaning tables, a pool, and laundry facilities. For those traveling with children, there are game rooms and a recreation room where movies are shown.

From this location, you can easily access the Atlantic side of Big Pine Key and venture around the south side of the island, where you will find a rocky, sandy coastline, very remote except for a few private residences and three bed-and-breakfast inns. This strip of land is called Long Beach. You can continue on to explore the Newfound Harbor Keys and Coupon Bight. See the description below.

To reach the inns by land, turn left off U.S. 1 onto Long Beach Road. On the Atlantic side you will find the **Casa Grande** (305-872-2878), **Barnacle Bed and Breakfast** (305-872-3298), and **Deer Run** (305-872-2015). They do not have public accesses for kayakers.

You may also find **easy access put-ins** along Long Beach Drive to Coupon Bight. There are several areas accessible for kayaking. One in particular is quite remote, and four-wheel drive vehicles are best suited for passage over the rough terrain. This site is found south along Long Beach Drive. You will come into a curve about half a mile past Big Pine Key Fishing Lodge. Just as you come out of the curve, there is a bumpy road on the right that goes perpendicular to Long Beach Drive. Go slowly over this uneven terrain until you come to the hard-packed fill, about one hundred yards past the curve. Veer left and you will find **accessible water (site 2-B)** for your kayak on the north or west end of the clearing.

Further along Long Beach Drive, in the residential section, there are **three small put-ins** hidden along the right side of the road. The first one is about six-tenths of a mile from the lodge, where stone columns grace both sides of Long Beach Road. On the right, in front of the column marked "Long Beach Estates," there is a clearing in the shrubs where you can put in **(site 2-C)**. Be careful; this site is a little muddy, and putting in, as well as recovering, could be a little messy. You will find the next launch about nine-tenths of a mile from the lodge opposite a house **(site 2-D)**. You may have to look carefully where the buttonwood trees have been broken away. Rocks near the shoulder of the road provide a narrow break in the shoreline. The last site down the road is a shallow wooden launch and may be more difficult to find. It is 1.6 miles from the lodge **(site 2-E)**. All of these sites may prove challenging during the lower tides associated with mid-winter months. You can park your vehicle along the shoulder of Long Beach Road when using each.

All of these sites will give you easy access to shallow grassy flats and small mangrove islands, abundant with wading birds as well as small sharks and stingrays. During the winter months, this area is a popular rookery for many migrating aquatic birds. For this reason, this area is now a state aquatic preserve. North of the mangrove areas is a protected basin called Coupon Bight. This basin is ideal for days when weather is less than favorable for open water exploration.

Beyond the southern point of Big Pine Key, a group of small islands called the Newfound Harbor Keys jut westward. Waterways that pass between these islands are usually shallow and are accessible only during high tides. West of Coupon Bight and north of the Newfound Harbor Keys is a protected harbor called Newfound Harbor. Popular for years with live-aboards, the area has several marinas. Powerboat traffic can be a little overwhelming at times, so use caution when using open water routes.

A shallow coral reef is located about a quarter mile from shore in about 10 feet of water. On days when the weather is favorable, this is a popular dive spot for locals and visitors, with the most activity occurring near a red marker 50. This is called a day marker because it is not lighted for night-time navigation. An anchor is not necessary here because there are mooring buoys to secure your kayaks while you dive. Many species of tropical fish visit this patch reef, and it is home to hundreds of small sergeant majors, parrot fish, angels, grunts, chubs, and jacks, to name only a few. The coral patch reefs run parallel to these islands as far down as Cook Island. Mooring buoys are not provided at these other locations. At the south end of this chain of small islands, you will find an exclusive resort. **Little Palm Island**, a four-star **resort**, caters to the likes of movie stars and vice-presidents. You can go ashore if you have reservations for **dining**. The restaurant opened to the general public in 1997, serving three meals every day of the week. It is by far one the prettiest places to eat in all the Florida Keys (305-872-2524).

Gulf side of Big Pine Key

Once you've spent any time in the lower Keys, you start to see the simplicity of the islands. Big Pine Key is no exception. U.S. 1 just grazes the southern portion of the island. A person driving along U.S. 1 sees little of Big Pine Key, and so might not realize that it's the second largest island in the Keys by area. But to the north of that driver, large portions of undisturbed Caribbean slash pine, which gave Big Pine Key its name, are just moments off the busy highway. Also abundant here are silver and thatch palms and poisonwood. Poisonwood produces an oil that can cause a rash much like poison ivy. Orchids, cactus, and air plants add to the variety of plants found here. There are at least 466 species of plants on Big Pine alone. This area makes up the heart and soul of the National Key Deer Wildlife Refuge. Turning at the traffic light off U.S. 1 and taking either fork, you will begin to see the vastness of the island.

The right fork, Wilder Road, winds through a residential area to a famous pizza eatery, the **No Name Pub** (305-872-9115). Across the street from the commercial lobster and crab trap yard is the **Old Wooden Bridge Fish Camp** (305-872-2241), location for the filming of many small movies and television commercials in recent years. It gets its name from the bridge that runs from Big Pine over to No Name Key (although the bridge isn't wooden anymore). No Name Key is one of the few islands here that is independent of the city water and electric system. It uses water cisterns and solar energy. The left fork off U.S. 1 is Key Deer Boulevard, where a good number of the tiny deer are seen, especially in the early morning and early evening hours. This fork takes you out near the northern point of Big Pine Key. Here, a remote launch site provides access to several attractions worthy of viewing during exploration of the Gulf side of Big Pine Key and neighboring islands.

The Blue Hole is three miles from the intersection of U.S. 1 and Key Deer Boulevard. It is on the left and is clearly marked by a state sign. Kayaking is not allowed; however, it is a site to admire. Soon after the completion of the construction of U.S. 1, this rock quarry filled with fresh water from rainfall. It is now home to Florida soft-shell turtles, the endangered Key mud turtles, red-eared turtles, yellow-bellied skimmer turtles, and box turtles. Also on hand are the resident alligators. For hikers there is a viewing platform and a walking trail with flora description markers.

Further down, a trail clearly marked on the highway by state sign, the Jack Watson Nature Trail, bordering Watson's Hammock, offers the hiking enthusiast a vast array of vegeta-

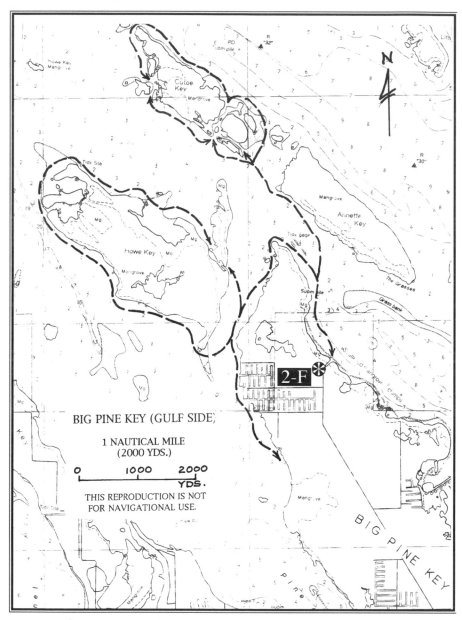

Big Pine Key (Gulf Side)

tion found throughout the lower Keys, some found only on Big Pine Key. The trail is dedicated to Jack Watson, whose father homesteaded the Watson's Hammock area in 1905. The elder Watson received a deed for 107 acres in the hammock. Mrs. Watson sold the property to the North American Wildlife Foundation, who in turn gave it to the U.S. Fish and Wildlife Service as part of the Key Deer National Wildlife Refuge. The son, Jack Watson, was the first state enforcement officer ever hired to control the poaching of deer. In 1951 he became the first refuge manager. The nature trail itself was established in 1957.

The environment can be harsh. Tide waters sometimes flood the foot trail leading to the Indian mounds, making passage somewhat slippery. Marsh grasses can scratch your ankles, and mosquitoes can be relentless in the rainy season (June through September). Rattlesnakes can also be found in this area; be careful where you step. During long periods of outdoor exposure, be sure to use a strong sun block on your skin, wear a hat, and carry insect repellent. Feeding or molesting deer or any wildlife is prohibited. Refuge hours are one-half hour before sunrise to one-half hour after sunset.

You can kayak to a remote portion of this preserve where Native Americans once lived and where their ancient middens now lie. No archaeological digs have ever been allowed at this site, and it is protected from vandals by the vigilance of the community members and officers of the park.

When you drive to the end of Key Deer Boulevard, just past the Lion's Club, you will find a narrow trail leading off to the right, about one hundred feet before the road ends. Follow the trail some fifty yards into a large clearing where you will find a shallow canal. From here you can easily **launch (site 2-F)** toward the north. There are many areas of interest to the kayaker.

If you round the point of Big Pine Key and continue south

along the west coast, you will pass over shallow tidal areas and be able to explore an array of life. After a mile or so, you will pass Port Pine Heights, a residential housing area. There are canals that give passage to small boats. Please use caution in and around these canals, as well as all along the waterfront of this area, because powerboat traffic is common. Continue past this development, and again you will find undisturbed woodlands with a coastal mangrove region. This is the Watson's Hammock area. Continue for some 1200 yards past the development. You will find a boat basin and a modest residence sitting alone in the woods. This is private property. Five hundred yards further south is a narrow break in the mangroves where there is hard bottom. Look closely for this opening in the mangrove prop roots. Whenever possible, try not to disturb the natural growth around the mangrove habitat. Tie your kayak up very carefully to the mangroves and walk shoreward. The trail is only five to ten yards from the shoreline and is very easy to find.

You follow the trail for about a mile until it ends at a heavily wooded area. These are the middens of the Calusa Indians. Large trees, mostly gumbo limbo, grow majestically out of the center of most of these mounds. Piled all about the area are horse conch and queen conch shells, in pieces and whole. The conchs were once a source of food for the early inhabitants of Big Pine Key. *Please do not remove these or any plant life from this area!* The public is invited to explore this unique place, but your respect and cooperation will determine whether or not future generations will be allowed such privileges. The Wildlife Refuge management asks that you do not enter this area between April 1 and May 31, because this is when the key deer are foaling.

Another trip leaving from **launch site 2-F** incorporates the islands of Annette Key, Cuttoe Key, and Howe Key. Annette Key, found northeast of the northern point of Big Pine Key, offers little except good cover from a fierce northeast wind

Hidden tidal passages can offer access to seldom-explored lagoons, like this one on Big Munson's Island.

during the winter months while traveling north to Cuttoe Key. Cuttoe Key has some of the first narrow tidal creeks you will find in this part of the lower Keys. On the south end of the island, there are several scattered mangrove islands, apart from the main body of Cuttoe Key. It is here that you get a firsthand look at what the tide can do over time to these shallow relief areas. Many birds, including ospreys, make their nests here in the winter months. You can find large schools of mullet, accompanied by sharks and rays in these narrow tide creeks. There may be some difficulty in accessing this area during the winter months at low tide, for the grass flats surrounding the island are very shallow and offer little water even for the kayaker. Tide adjustment should be approximately one hour later than the Content Keys adjustment. (See the table in the section on Tides and Weather.)

The last area of interest to us in this section is Howe Key. This island is relatively large and has a shallow basin on three sides. Howe Key also has dry land, but the Wildlife Refuge officials ask that you don't go ashore without permission. Permits are not given for recreational use at this time but are issued mainly for research. Rattlesnakes, scorpions, Key deer, and raccoons are frequent visitors to this important offshore island. These shallow basins, like most in this area, are difficult to access at low tide and can have bottom features from muddy flats to hard, sharp bottoms. Please use caution in and around these areas.

3. The Torch Keys

(Including Middle and Big Torch Keys)

In this chapter, we will explore several groups of islands entirely on the Gulf side of the Keys. This calm area is ideal for the novice kayaker and offers an opportunity to the experienced kayaker on days when the weather may not be so cooperative. Easily accessed and very protected, these islands can offer a daylong adventure with little exposure to harsh winds. However, tides may be a consideration. On warm sunny days during the summer months, this course could prove a bit stifling.

Middle and Big Torch Keys

Traveling south on U.S. 1, just after Little Torch Key, you pass mile marker 28 on the Torch Channel Bridge. The next island is Middle Torch Key. On the left side of the highway is a sign pointing toward the right, down a road that runs perpendicular to U.S. 1. This is the way to Big Torch Key. For the most part, the drive is quiet with little traffic. After driving almost 2.5 miles north, you come to a "Big Torch Key" sign pointing left. Turn left onto the wooded road. This road is unlike any other in the lower Keys. The vegetation here is scrubby, consisting mostly of hardwoods like buttonwood, stopper trees, poisonwood, and black bead. This wooded area is very dense, unlike the other wooded areas of Big Pine Key, where the vegetation is taller and thinner. A short distance down this straightaway is a causeway with water on both

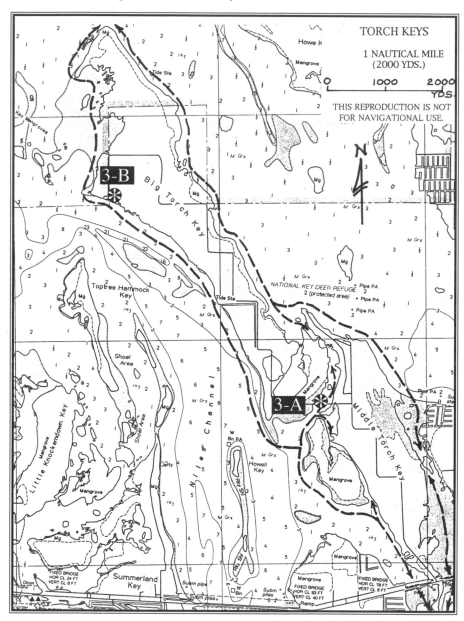

The Torch Keys

sides. On the left, approaching the causeway, there is a place for parking that looks south toward Niles Channel Bridge. Parking on the causeway is also permitted.

The only decision to make at this easily accessible **launch site (3-A)** is whether to put in on the south side or the north side, depending on which area you want to explore. From the south side, you can easily access the Niles Channel side of Big Torch Key and navigate the neighboring islands. In the event there is a north-northeast wind, you can stay in the lee of the island, hugging the west side of Big Torch Key. When you travel north toward the Gulf, your route is protected until you turn the corner and start down the windward side. Keep in mind that during a south wind, usually occurring during the late winter or early spring months, the opposite is true. See the description later in this chapter of the put-in at the terminus of this road for a trip that allows you to avoid this problem.

From the causeway launch site, you can also explore close to shore the area of Middle Torch Key toward the bridge. Pass under the bridge and return between Little Torch Key and Middle Torch Key. The areas between these two islands are shallow and very muddy, but passage can be made easily. During the midwinter months, especially associated with very windy cold fronts, wading birds come into this area to take advantage of the shallows that make feeding easy.

Accessing the north side of the causeway allows you to explore both the Pine Channel side and a shallow cut between Big Torch Key and Middle Torch Key. On the northwest end of Big Torch Key are the Torch Key mangroves. This is an excellent site to explore the hard bottom community. You can also observe numerous aquatic birds in good numbers and varieties foraging these shallow flats for food. In the mangroves furthest out near Niles Channel, you may find a popular rookery where birds await the next opportunity to feed on the falling tide or to rest for the night.

From your launch site at the causeway, the trip around Big Torch Key is 8 miles. The route that follows Middle Torch Key, passes between this island and Little Torch Key, and returns to the causeway is just over 6 miles.

You can get another perspective on this area by following Big Torch Road across the causeway and driving for 5 more miles. Along the way you pass one sparsely populated residential area with outcroppings of "dwarf mangrove" trees of both black and red varieties. The road ends facing south. You can park a vehicle in the turn-around. By following a foot path leading straight away from the terminated road, you will discover an opening where tide waters bathe a shallow pool. With a short portage, you can easily **access** this tide pool **(site 3-B)**. Be careful of the sharp rocks and sudden muddy depressions.

This area is a little more forgiving during southern winds which blow through the Keys during the early spring or late winter months. By following the coast south toward U.S. 1, you will be able to make good time against the wind. The island gives you an adequate lee on its west side. Along the way, you will pass a few docks and private residences. About halfway down, or about a mile and a half, there is a canal. The mouth of this canal provides an area to rest out of the wind. Continue south for another mile and a half, and there you will find the passage between Big and Middle Torch Keys. Turn east and paddle toward the causeway that connects the two islands. (You drove over this causeway to get onto Big Torch Key and to launch site 3-B. It is also the site of launch 3-A.) Rest briefly and portage your kayak across the short span of land. Continue downwind along the east side of Big Torch Key for the remaining trip to the launch site, about 6 miles. Finding this remote launch site from your kayak could be tricky if you do not pay attention, especially if it gets dark before you can return. Make a mental note of where it is before you depart, or mark the entrance to the lagoon with something recognizable, like a rag or dive flag. Round trip around Big Torch Key is about 9 miles.

In the summer months, you may prefer to use the areas away from the narrow passes and more to the open water where cooler air and waters are found. In a later chapter of this book, we will also use launch site 3-B to access the area of Content Key.

4. Summerland Key

(Including Little Knockemdown Key and Toptree Hammock Key)

The Gulf side of Summerland Key and the neighboring islands of Toptree Hammock and Little Knockemdown Keys offer shallow waters excellent for viewing hard bottom as well as soft bottom communities and is also recommended for viewing aquatic birds. Appropriate for novice kayakers, this area is very forgiving during windy conditions regardless of the wind's direction. However, tides should be considered. Although the course is ideal for the novice, the more advanced kayaker can find this area challenging also by undertaking the entire course. It is an excellent area for a mixed group.

Leaving the Torch Keys, drive south along U.S. 1 over the Niles Channel Bridge to Summerland Key at mile marker 25. Turning right just past Monte's Restaurant, drive to the second right, and turn right again. After about 200 yards, turn left onto Niles Road, which concludes after a mile and a half drive north. At the end, you will find a gate on your right and open water on your left. This **launch site (4-A)** is easily accessed and there is plenty of parking on the shoulder of the road just before its terminus. Please don't block the gate; it is a private entrance.

This island is populated largely on the Atlantic side, leaving the Gulf side somewhat undisturbed. In this area, the rocky shoals offer an opportunity to view such marine animals as stingrays and sharks, as well as many species of inverte-

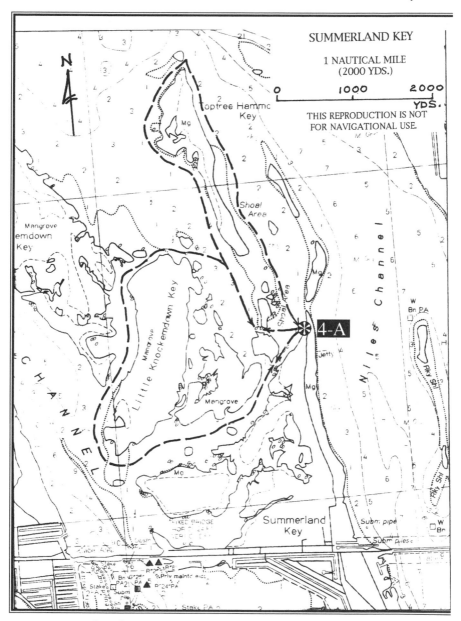

A peaceful, easy access for kayaking can be found at the end of Niles Road, Summerland Key.

brates, marine sponges, and crustaceans. Low tide is an ideal time to view aquatic birds of numerous species as they feed on exposed tidal flats.

The island groups for primary exploration from this put-in are Toptree Hammock Key to the north, Little Knockemdown Key to the west, and the Summerland Key mangroves toward Kemp Channel to the south. There are many ways to work this area, but the wind direction should determine your selection. Whenever possible, start out with the wind facing you, so that your return is easier when you are tired. The course will be outlined to accommodate a north wind; for a south wind, the reverse of the outlined course would be best.

Departing the launch and heading west, you will soon pass between two small mangrove outcrops about 500 yards out. A shoal on the north side runs up into Toptree Hammock Key. Once through the pass, there is easily navigable water. From here, you should determine which course of action to take.

Following this rocky shoal north, you can pass along the west side of Toptree Hammock Key, stay in the lee of the island away from the wind until you round the north point of the island, and return downwind to the launch. This course is about 4.5 miles or 8000 yards.

You can also head in a northwesterly direction and round the island of Little Knockemdown Key, passing downwind between Little and Big Knockemdown Keys. There is a shoal as you turn southwest between the two islands. You may find this a sticky spot at low tide. Once you clear this shoal, deep water should resume until you reach the southwest point of Little Knockemdown Key. Follow the shoal out on a southwest course until you round a small mangrove island some 300 yards past the main body of Little Knockemdown Key. Turning now to the east, continue through the main pass between Little Knockemdown Key and Summerland Key. This will lead back to the launch site. This course is about 5 miles or 9000 yards.

Leda's Bridge is one of the many quaint surprises that can be found on Summerland Key.

The islands of Toptree Hammock Key and Little Knockemdown Key are unique and quite different from each other. Toptree Hammock Key is off-limits to people because it is an important wildlife habitat, like most islands on the Gulf side of the lower Keys. The east side of Toptree Hammock has a hard, shallow bottom where marine sponges and other invertebrates can be seen. The west side is shallow, grassy, and often muddy. It is an excellent place for viewing nurse and lemon sharks, as well as stingrays. The west side is also good for viewing aquatic birds at low tide.

Little Knockemdown Key, on the other hand, is a private island that is divided into parcels for sale to individuals. A few homes and docks will be seen as you venture around the island. Please respect the privacy of others.

5. Cudjoe Key

(Including Knockemdown Key)

The two trips covered in this section are excellent trips for the warm summer months, as well as calm winter days. These trips could prove challenging for even an experienced kayaker in strong winds. Both are about the same length, roughly 4.5 miles. They can easily be done together in the same outing by more experienced kayakers.

Leaving Summerland Key and driving south along the Overseas Highway (U.S. 1), you cross over Kemp Channel Bridge onto Cudjoe Key. Looking northeast to your far right, you can see Knockemdown Key. Looking northwest, you may see a peculiar sight. Two large white blimps, one that is usually tethered to the ground, appear just over the trees.

I think it is important to understand the significance of these anomalies that seem to invade an otherwise pristine habitat. The blimp base is a government facility, largely civilian-staffed, and generally quiet. One of the blimps is used to detect low-flying aircraft bound for the U.S. from South and Central America. The other is a broadcast tower for transmitting *Radio Martí* for Cuban citizens living in Cuba. *Radio Martí* is designed as a window to the world and gives native Cubans uncensored news and programming. The transmitting blimp is usually deployed in the early morning hours, weather permitting. Whether the blimps are on the surface or aloft, they point into the wind. For this reason either blimp at ground level can help you to determine wind direction before, or any-

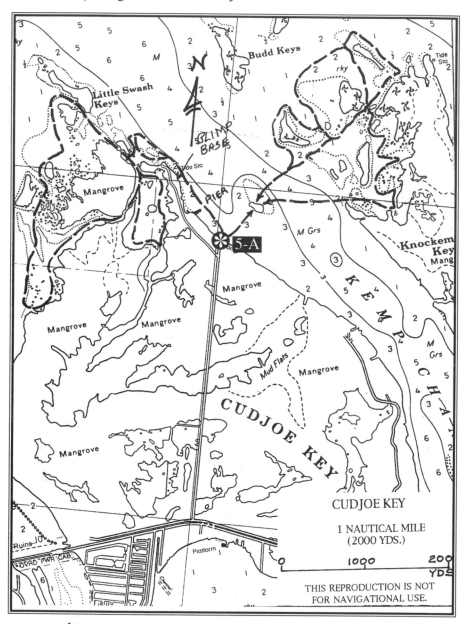

Cudjoe Key

time after, you set out. This is very helpful because this area is open to strong and changeable winds from all directions. I have many times started out with the wind favoring one direction, then later had to correct the course to compensate for the changing wind.

One-half mile past mile marker 22, turn right on Blimp Road and drive 2 miles to its end. This **launch site (5-A)** is a county boat ramp. From here you can look north into the open Gulf that is just past the islands in the distance. The blimp base is northwest up the coast. Knockemdown Key is to the immediate east.

It is here that I start many of my kayak tours. I have launched with thousands of customers who returned satisfied, if not somewhat tired, after three-hour excursions through the tidal basins of Knockemdown Key, among the tidal basins immediately behind the blimp base, and out to Bow Channel. This area has a wonderful access advantage. plenty of parking, remoteness, and quiet except for some activity at the blimp base.

Because this launch site is so exposed, extreme caution should be used on windier days. More advanced kayakers will find this course a challenge because there are endless possibilities for territories to explore. The shallow tidal basins offer the novice the feeling of being alone with nature's splendor.

Knockemdown Key

If you intend to kayak toward the open water north or to Knockemdown Key, the small island northeast of the launch, some 600 yards out, should be your first destination. The island is often full of roosting aquatic birds, some even nesting in the winter months. On group trips, this island offers a final chance to be sure that everyone is comfortable with his/her obligation before going any farther, a kind of "shakedown" if you will. At this point you can determine the effect of the wind on selected routes. From here, the protected basins of Knockemdown Key are 800 yards away.

During the winter months, there is usually a wind blowing on the north side of the islands, either from the north or the east. It is very easy to use this to your advantage. By heading north to enter the island during an east wind, you will return with the wind behind you later. The opposite is true for a north wind. Head east and return downwind from the north to the launch. This tidal basin, located entirely on the northwest corner of Knockemdown Key, is affected by the tides. At low tides, take care when working the basin.

When you approach Knockemdown Key from either direction, the area you want to explore is not immediately evident because the basin is nearly enclosed by the island itself. Two small tidal passages, not much wider at low tide than the kayak itself, are often the basin's only access. This basin is delightfully alive with an impressive display of sea grasses, colorful marine sponges, invertebrates, fish and crabs. You glide over water that often looks sparkling clear and is only a few inches deep!

Schools of bait fish often attract an impressive display of wading aquatic birds and diving raptors (osprey). At high tide, it is common to see even the larger sharks, some 6 feet long, cruising the interior basin in search of food. They can be a most imposing display from the kayak.

To find this remote marine world, you can enter from the north side by heading northeast from the small island mentioned earlier, across grass flats so shallow that few power boats can cross, and find a troughlike channel, paralleling this first island of the Knockemdown set. Heading northeast, follow the hard light bottom through a small pass that leads into the interior basin. Now surrounding you is indeed a wonderful site. Isolated from the outside world and as quiet as a hospital ward, Knockemdown reveals its beauty.

You can also approach this basin by heading east across Kemp Channel from the small island, until you encounter the rocky shoreline of Knockemdown Key. Make your way north along the coast until you find an opening in the islands that takes you inward over hard bottom, across beautifully colored sponges, and through a shallow tidal stream into the interior basin. This entrance is easier at low tide than the one on the north end of Knockemdown Key.

Whether you approach from the north or the east, you will find hours of undisturbed solitude. In my many trips here, I have seldom met with other people or even evidence of them in the form of drifting debris. By exploring the many smaller tidal basins within this great area, you can discover for yourself why I choose this site as my premier trip.

Next we will explore the area between the north end of Cudjoe Key and the Little Swash Keys. The avid kayaker may want to continue on to this area after kayaking Knockemdown. If you wish to do so, cross Kemp Channel from the north end of Knockemdown and head west toward the break in the islands between Cudjoe and Little Swash Keys. From there, you can enjoy this wonderful maze of tidal-fed basins and tide streams.

Cudjoe Key

After exploring the wonders that make up Knockemdown Key, you can explore another habitat from the same launch site. Looking northwest up the coast toward the blimp base, you can see a wooden pier jutting away from the base about 600 yards from the launch. Just as the island in the channel was a shakedown for Knockemdown Key, this pier can serve the same function as you work out any problems between the launch and the pier before going any further. The base is a military installation and access is restricted. Please make no attempt to land on the base site. As you round the pier, you will get a firsthand look at the huge dirigibles. They are an imposing sight up close. After rounding the blimp station, continue up the coast northward. On calmer days you can

A serene mid-afternoon kayak trip through a tidal basin off Cudjoe Key offers schooling mangrove snappers, small sharks, and feeding birds.

view again the impressive display of sponges just out from the coastline. This display of unique marine animals continues for about 300 yards past the blimp. About two hundred yards past the blimp, looking left where the islands break, you will find a passage where there are signs warning of entry onto the base. It is okay to enter by waterway, just not by land. Often this passage is too shallow for even kayaks to cross. An alternative is to continue up the coast for another 200 yards, where the next small group of mangroves ends, and start inside from there. On extreme low tides this passage may seem too shallow as well. Take your time and slowly work over this shallow spot, for sufficient water awaits on the other side. Turning south back toward the base, through a narrow creek, you will now find ample water. You will also start to see the effects of the tide. Tidal flow through this narrow passage is affected by the constant filling and draining of the basin to the south. When the tide is incoming, the water flows from Kemp Channel, through this tide stream, and into the shallow basin. On an outgoing tide, the opposite is true. This passage offers a splendid site of marine activity. Gray (mangrove) snapper enjoy the faster moving water caused by the bottle-neck effect the mangrove roots have on the tide water. Long strands of turtle and manatee grass break the surface of the water, offering shelter to the many fish and crabs that call this small wonder home. Schools of small gray snapper hide around the root formations or around an occasional rocky ledge. At times, hundreds of these ghostlike fish can be seen in this one small area.

Soon the mangroves give way again to the awesome view of the blimps and to a tidal basin unlike any other in the lower Keys. Moving southeast, toward the base, you begin to notice that the tidal current subsides, becoming almost nonexistent. Shallow grass flats give way to juvenile red mangroves, hud-dled together. Small lemon and nurse sharks and brown rays are common sights. These flats are feeding grounds for numerous aquatic birds.

Before exploring any further, notice the coastline on your right, when facing the blimps. This is the way out of the basin without repeating the way in. The passage curves around to the west, and through another tidal creek before spilling out into Bow Channel. Take note of its location before venturing into the basin, for later, it may not be so apparent. You will also notice that the current is flowing the opposite direction from what you first observed upon entering the basin.

Take some time and explore the basin, especially if there is enough water to cross over the main body toward the small island in the middle. Because of the shallowness here, birds can be observed feeding almost any time of the day. The tidal flow makes this area abundant with small fish that attract flocks of these wading, long-legged wonders. The island in the middle of the basin is unique. It is in fact two small mangrove islands that have grown together to form what looks like one. Upon closer examination, you will find a passage that goes between the two islands, offering a unique look at the interior workings of the mangrove habitat.

After exploring the protected basin, you can exit out the west side, as mentioned earlier. You will notice again a tidal effect, and this will indicate that you are on the way out. In the narrow portion, you will probably experience the most tidal current. Then it will soon diminish to slower moving water. This wide tidal creek will empty into Bow Channel and from here you can explore south toward the highway or north back to the launch. To the south, you will follow an almost unbroken coast as it leads you toward Bow Channel Bridge. After about a mile or so, you should double back along the outside of Cudjoe Key. I have often encountered larger sharks along the hard, broken bottom through this area. It can be well

Narrow tidal passages can be difficult to find for the first time, like this tidal passage on the north end of Cudjoe Key.

worth exploring. Small mangrove outcrops, as well as larger islands with tidal accesses between them, will dot the way north. Being careful to stay off shoals, you can weave your way through these passes if the water is sufficient, or go around Little Swash Keys, and start your way back toward the launch in ample water. Along this west side, neighboring Bow Channel, between Cudjoe Key and Little Swash Key, I have observed one of the largest colonies of shore birds (terns, dowitchers and turnstones, to name a few) perching in the short mangrove community. These birds, by their sheer numbers, have caused the trees to be flattened, like bonsai trees. They are most abundant during the high tide, for at low tide they are often out feeding.

6. Sugarloaf Key

(Including Perky Creek, Five-mile Creek,
Sammy's Creek)

J ust over the bridge from Cudjoe Key, driving south
along U.S. 1, you pass over the Bow Channel Bridge
and onto the first of the Sugarloaf Keys. Further south are the
Saddlebunch Keys. This section will cover both groups of
islands.

The island of Sugarloaf Key is shaped like a boomerang.
Starting just northwest of Cudjoe Key, Sugarloaf Key extends
south into the Atlantic and west toward Key West until it joins
the Saddlebunch Keys. It has an impressive mangrove coastline, largely uninhabited on the Atlantic side. On the north
side of the "boomerang" lie shallow tidal basins, very large in
area and ideal for the novice or for an experienced kayaker on
days when the weather makes open passages difficult. An
added attraction in this area are indigenous tidal creeks that
offer a unique look at the red mangrove habitat. Teeming with
life from the Atlantic as well as the Gulf of Mexico, they offer
an exciting contrast between the two bodies of water.
Running as deep as 20 feet and as shallow as a few inches,
they can have tremendous currents running through them as
well.

Upper Sugarloaf Key

Upper Sugarloaf Key is the most northern of the Sugarloaf
group, directly across the Bow Channel Bridge. In Upper
Sugarloaf Key, there are **four launch sites** and **two camping**

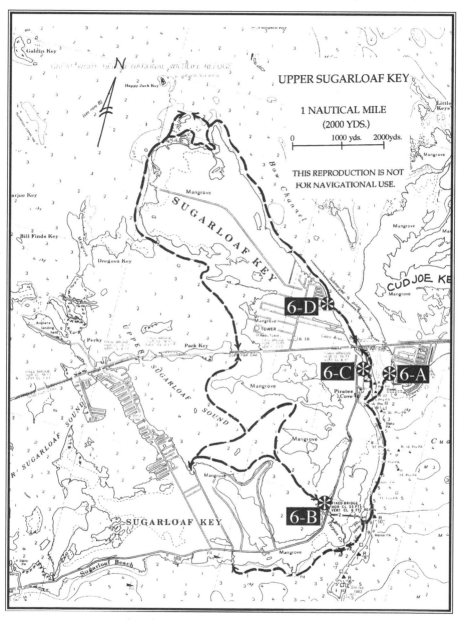

Upper Sugarloaf Key

facilities. The launch sites can conveniently place you near the area you wish to explore; however, one of them is very remote, and passenger cars and trailers may find it difficult to access.

The **first launch site (6-A)** is on the Cudjoe Key side of Bow Channel. Traveling southbound on U.S. 1, pass mile marker 21. Turn left on Drost Street and drive to the end. You will find a quaint marina called Cudjoe Key Marina across Bow Channel and north a bit from Tarpon Creek. Launching from here costs $8, but it keeps you off the main road. Heading out through the canal, you pass a wonderful, small mangrove island with an abundance of wading birds. Crossing Bow Channel and following the coast of Sugarloaf Key south about 1.5 miles, you will soon see where the mangroves give way to the tide water. Head inland through the mangroves. The first creek that you will see is well marked and used quite frequently by power boaters and jet skiers.

The next creek, less active than the first, is Tarpon Creek, located down the coast toward an apparent bulge in the island 4000 yards east of Sugarloaf Beach. Large mangrove trees give the entrance an almost haunted look as you paddle toward the interior of the island. Keep your eyes open for finger creeks that can be explored as well. These finger creeks offer the kayaker a challenging opportunity to explore narrow, dead-end passes under the trees. You feel a sense of discovery since these creeks are seldom explored by other boaters. Soft, silty bottom gives way to hard sponge-covered bottom as you move along. Unfortunately, this particular creek has a sizable amount of trash and debris around the mangrove roots.

If you follow the main artery, you will pass the main intersection of all the creeks in this system. (This intersection is also the location of launch site 6-B below.) There are the remains of a burned-out highway bridge that once carried the first automobiles into the lower Keys, and ultimately into Key

Sunrise is a beautiful time in the Great White Heron Refuge as twilight turns to daylight.

West. This bridge is out and so ends the road going south. There is neither automobile traffic nor inhabitant anywhere on the other side. Continuing along the creek, you will find that it spills out into a large tidal basin. This is called Upper Sugarloaf Sound. This is a beautifully protected, shallow lagoon worthy of exploration.

The basin spreads out toward the northwest, through a break in two points of land. If you look northwest, you can see the main highway through a break in the islands. Once you pass between the points, you will start to see residential houses to the southwest. If you go through the pass on the northwest and follow the coastline on the left (south) side, you will also find a long, straight canal that was dredged many years ago, when this kind of activity was allowed. By following it south to the open Atlantic, you can make this a round trip and return to the launch by going east up the coast. The round trip distance is about 6.5 miles.

As mentioned earlier in this section, you still have several choices of **launch sites**. First, cross over the Bow Channel Bridge traveling south past mile marker 20. Turn left and drive 500 yards to the entrance of the Sugarloaf KOA **campground**. Second, continue on this road (939, or S.R. 4) past the KOA for 2 more miles over a rough, unmaintained roadway to the end, where the road concludes at the burned-out bridge. **There is a place on the right side where you can launch a kayak (6-B)**. You may also use the **launch ramp at the campground (6-C)**, but there is a $10 fee for non-guests. For guests, the ramp is free. Either of these sites provides easy access to Tarpon Creek and Upper Sugarloaf Sound. There is another **campground** next to the KOA called Lazy Lakes, but it has no water access.

For exploring the northern Gulf side of Sugarloaf Key, there is a ramp located in a residential section. There is no charge to launch here. To find this **launch site (6-D)**, drive south past mile marker 20 about one-half mile and turn right on Crane Boulevard. You will see a sign saying Sugarloaf Elementary and Middle School. Drive north on Crane past the school. Turn right on Seminole Street, then left on Cherokee Street. Finally, turn right on Aztec. At the end of Aztec, you will see the launch ramp. There is parking along the side of the ramp.

From here, you can easily explore the north side of the island for several miles. The northern tip of the island has a large tidal flat. This flat is rocky and is largely exposed during low tide, an opportune time to observe birds and other marine life in action. During windier conditions, this site could prove challenging. You can then round the north end of Upper Sugarloaf Key. Pass between Upper Sugarloaf Key and Dreguez Key, and travel south through Upper Sugarloaf Sound. Continuing south, pass under either Park Channel Bridge, North Harris Bridge, or Harris Gap Bridge. You can then either continue south through the long straight channel and work east along the coast to your return, or head south-east toward Tarpon Creek and start your return. During

116

windier conditions, this course could prove challenging. This course is about 12 miles as a round trip and would be a full day's outing, but there are several places along the way to take breaks.

Lower Sugarloaf Key

If ever there were a kayaker's paradise in the Florida Keys, it is here. Lower Sugarloaf Key offers something for every skill level and any weather condition. Within this small area, there are three very exciting trips; however, there are a few distractions you should note. First, you are going to be accessing near U.S. 1, and the sound of cars may be heard at all times during these trips. Second, NAS Boca Chica, the Naval Air Base near Key West, flies its fighter aircraft frequently over these areas. Third, jet skis and small powerboats can be seen and heard throughout these areas. By no means should you let these distractions interfere with your adventures. Snorkeling is recommended in and around some of these areas as outlined later in this section.

Perky Creek

Our first point of interest should be a rather small tidal creek located north of Lower Sugarloaf Key and on the south side of Upper Sugarloaf Sound. The easiest access is at **Sugarloaf Key Marina**, located in the Sugarloaf Lodge Complex. Traveling south from Upper Sugarloaf Key, you drive through Park Key and then over another small island. After mile marker 18, you're on Lower Sugarloaf Key. Six hundred yards past the bridge, you will see a fire station on the right next to a convenience store. Around back is Sugarloaf Key Marina. This small marina has groceries, rental boats, and fuel. You will also see a sizable complement of kayaks in the back by the ramp. They belong to a tour operator in Key West. This area is frequently used for kayak tours. You can **launch (6-E)** here for $1 (per kayak).

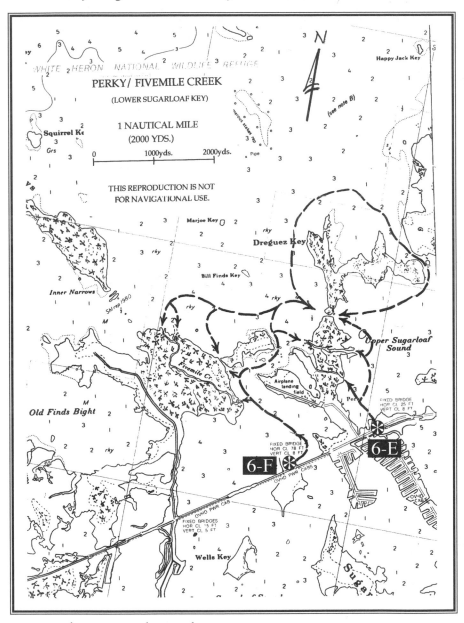

Perky/Five-mile Creek

Looking north when you launch, you will see open water on your right. There is a protected bight on your left. On windier days, you may want to follow the coast along the bight, thus avoiding a beating. Otherwise, you can go straight out to the point on the north end that is referred to as the Spider's Hole. This is a narrow creek, just big enough for a kayak, that cuts northwest through the mangroves. It gets its name because it is narrow enough for spiders to spin their webs across it, just above the tide waters — a good place to catch insects. These days this passage is used so frequently by kayakers that any webs that reach completion probably don't last long. After about a hundred yards, this creek widens, then adjoins Perky Creek. By taking Spider's Hole, you can avoid boat traffic from the marina and residential areas.

Use caution, especially during the winter months, when kayaking these creeks. Prevailing northern and northeastern winds strengthen the already strong currents. On the incoming tide you may find a good workout going out, but an easy return. On calmer days the wind and current are not as great a concern.

Perky Creek, like so many in the lower Keys, is abundant with small gray snapper and other common species of fish. Because of the tidal flow, marine sponges of many species can thrive on both the hard bottoms and the mangrove roots that dangle in the nourishing tide waters.

If you kayak northwest through any of the creeks around the Perky Creek area, you can then follow north along the coastline of Dreguez Key. The bottom is mostly shallow and hard. This area is ideal for viewing small sharks and rays, as well as nearshore game fish. This bottom is also habitat for marine sponges and other invertebrates. On windy days, kayaking along this coastline could prove challenging. You'll turn east as you round the northern tip of Dreguez Key, and a narrow passage between Dreguez and Upper Sugarloaf Keys will steer you back toward Sugarloaf Marina on a southwesterly course. Your round trip will be about 4.5 miles.

Alternatively, if you're a real enthusiast you can venture out toward Five-mile Creek by going west through any of the Perky Creek area passages, then following the coastline of the next island until you find an entrance to Five-mile Creek. You'll want to check the direction of the tide to help you decide whether to enter Five-mile Creek on its north end or its south end. A description of the Five-mile Creek trip follows.

Five-mile Creek

Northwest of Lower Sugarloaf Key lies an island between Old Finds Bight and Lower Sugarloaf Sound. The island has no name. The creek that divides it is not even close to 5 miles long, but it offers kayakers an exciting chance to explore one of the most unique formations between tides and mangroves. On the north end of the island, there is a Naval Communications Base displaying numerous towers.

You can launch from Sugarloaf Key Marina as mentioned in the last section, or you can **launch (6-F)** from U.S. 1 on the next island south of Lower Sugarloaf. Drive south past the Sugarloaf Lodge and mile marker 17. About 100 yards past the Harris Channel Bridge on the right side of the road, you will pass a 55 MPH speed limit sign. Turn carefully off the shoulder of the highway, and down the steep embankment you will find a clearing adjacent to the road. There is sufficient parking for three vehicles. Vehicles towing trailers should not attempt to launch from this site. Here, you can easily access the shallow water next to the narrow strip of land on the east side.

After launching, travel northwest for about three-quarters of a mile toward the closest point of the no-name island. Then follow the island north until you see a simple marker, usually made of PVC pipe with a buoy attached, which marks the entrance to the creek. You will at this point encounter a current, sometimes strong, flowing with or against your

Kayaking offers birdwatchers a unique perspective on their favorite pastime.

intended direction. If you find a swift current opposing, you may decide to keep going northeast and circle back to the west toward the towers, and then return through the creek downstream. If the tide is high, you can even take a shorter route by passing through a break in the island, just before the coast heads east. This could save a considerable amount of time, especially on a windy day. Whichever way you find easiest to gain entrance into the creek, what awaits you is well worth the effort.

In its protected cradle, the creek flows from Turkey Basin into Lower Sugarloaf Sound. These waters carry with them the necessary nourishment for life in our marine ecosystem. If entering from the north, you'll see deep, dark waters give way to muddy mangrove banks, carved by the very tide that offers opposition to the weary kayaker and covered in dozens of varieties of marine sponges that feed on the fertile waters flowing past them. Grass banks sway brilliantly where the tide

Sea Kayaking in the Florida Keys

Tidal waters give kayakers a gentle push while they enjoy scenery in the Florida Keys.

is slackened by wide berths in the tidal stream. Dangling prop roots, struggling to get a foothold on the muddy banks, offer protective cover to gray (mangrove) snapper. For a closer inspection of what lies below the surface, snorkeling is ideal on clear days. Be sure to display a diver's down flag, and be careful of boats passing through the creek. There are several smaller auxiliary creeks that can be used without disturbance. While snorkeling, be careful of the dangling roots and creek banks because they can have stinging organisms clinging to them. You can use lycra dive skins to avoid this problem. They can be rented from most dive shops for about $5. It is easiest to start your dive upstream and work down, keeping the kayak close by with a short piece of line.

Sugarloaf Creek (Sammy's Creek)

Sugarloaf Creek also feeds Lower Sugarloaf Sound, but its headwaters are the Atlantic. You can find this creek from the same **launch (6-F)** site as described for Five-mile Creek. You will need to pass under the Harris Channel Bridge and travel due south. You can also drive a little further, to just before mile marker 16, and **launch (6-G)** along U.S. 1 on the south side along the highway. There is enough room for parking without blocking the right-of-way. The course from this launch will be a little more southeasterly and take you through a little more open water.

As you set out, you will see a residential subdivision on your left. You will also see a undeveloped stretch of land directly in front of you. Set course for that remote stretch. Following the coast of Sugarloaf Key south, channel markers will veer to the right, leading you toward a system of creeks. The waters on the Lower Sugarloaf Sound side of the creeks are relatively shallow, with several deeper troughs that allow the passage of power boats. You can easily avoid these. The distance from the launch site to the creek system is 2 nautical miles (2.2 miles). An impressive tree line of red mangroves can be found where Sugarloaf Creek spills into the sound.

As at Five-mile Creek, there is one main artery of water that leads into the Atlantic. There are several smaller arteries that branch out from the main channel, all of which can all be explored by kayaks. Where the creek spills out into the Atlantic, there is a house set back off the bank. This is the Sammy residence where Joan Sammy has lived since 1953. The creek's nickname, Sammy's Creek, derives from her family name. If you see her out and about, stop and rest awhile and chat with her if you wish.

There is another portion of this sound that is very remote and can be accessed only by shallow draft vessels such as kayaks. From the Sugarloaf Sound side of the creeks, look to the east and follow the coastal mangroves for several hundred yards, until they turn south. Up ahead you will see a plot of land that certainly looks out of place. The land appears disturbed, and it is. During the Cuban Missile Crisis this was a

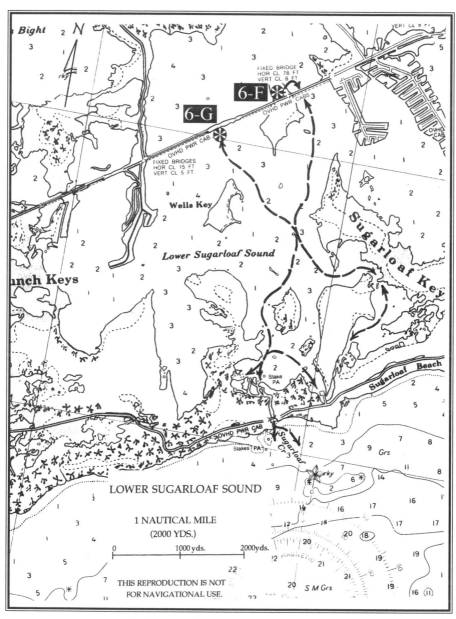

Lower Sugarloaf Sound

mobile launch site for missiles. It was hastily dredged and leveled to serve as the front line of defense in the event that things got ugly during this period. Now it serves more peaceful activities. Bee hives are found there. If you pass along the eastern side, there is a narrow divide in the trees that allows you to access the remote portion of the sound. There may not be sufficient water to pass over this shallow, sometimes exposed, passage. Seldom is it deeper than a foot and often it is shallower than 6 inches. I frequently use this remote passage on my kayak trips and have little problem, except during extreme low-water conditions in the winter months. If you follow the method described in the introduction, "Finding Your Way Around the Lower Keys," under the heading, "Portaging Your Kayak," you should have little problem. After a hundred yards or so, the passage is a little deeper and you can put the worst behind you as you travel northeast. For a while, the passage gets very narrow in places. Then all of a sudden, it breaks out into a lagoon again. On your right is a small opening. If you are quiet, you can often observe many species of the wading aquatic birds taking a midday nap. Your sudden appearance will certainly startle them. Moving on toward the northeast, the basin opens up even more, and you will find that the bottom here is mostly sand. You are on the Sugarloaf Sound side of Sugarloaf Beach. There are several handy shore breaks where you can rest. During the winter months, many birds enjoy the protected, calm waters offered by this lagoon as well as its bounty of mullet and other fish.

If you follow the coastline that you have been keeping on your left until it points north, you will soon pass through a narrow break in the islands. Continuing to follow the coastline to your left, you'll round a point to the left, then break out into the open water of Lower Sugarloaf Sound, where you will be able to see U.S. 1 again and make your way back to the launch, concluding a round trip of about 5 miles.

Sea Kayaking in the Florida Keys

All of the above mentioned trips are ideal during the winter months, when the weather is cooler. You should, however, consider other destinations during the summer months because the heat index in these closed basins can be stifling, especially during midday.

7. Boca Chica Key

(Including Geiger Key, Saddlehill Key, Bird Key, and Pelican Key)

I n this chapter we will discuss those areas closest to Key West that may hold interest to the kayaker. Though Key West trips do not offer the kayaker a peaceful setting, the areas mentioned here are very close to the island city and can be done with little planning and in very windy conditions. These areas are all on the Atlantic side of the islands and offer a different look at the lower Keys. These trips are located near Boca Chica Naval Air Station (NAS Boca Chica), and the continuous roar of jets and propeller aircraft can be heard. Local boat traffic in this area can also be heavy, and special care should be used when around the deeper chan nels. Please, don't let these facts discourage you, for this area is ideal for seeing firsthand the awesome strands of mangrove that neighbor the Atlantic side of the Keys.

Geiger Creek

Traveling south along U.S. 1 from the Saddlebunch Keys, just after mile marker 11, you cross the Shark Key Channel Bridge. Continuing south, you will soon pass a sign stating that you have now entered Big Coppitt Key. Shortly after the sign, there will be a left-hand turn. This is Boca Chica Road. Turning left, you will pass a Circle K convenience store on your right just off U.S. 1. This road runs south toward the Atlantic side of Boca Chica Key and ends after 3.5 miles, immediately behind the Naval Air Station. Here you will find

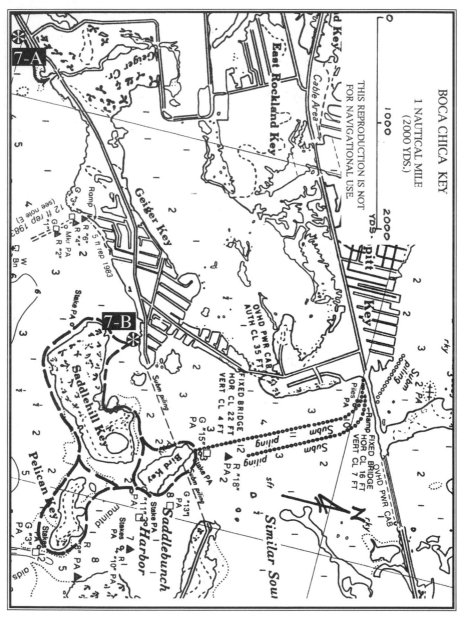

Boca Chica Key

a county beach, conveniently located for our first trip. There is usually ample parking along the shoulder of the road. Take a short jaunt down to the water's edge to **launch (7-A)** your kayak. During low tide, especially during the midwinter months, the water's edge could be out 100 feet or more from the dune. If, in fact, you observe this, take special care on this trip. Your outing could be a little more difficult because there are many shoals and muddy banks that are going to be exposed, creating obstacles for you to go around. On the other hand, this phenomena will certainly enhance the aquatic bird activity.

After launching, travel east up the coast. You will soon pass a quaint waterfront residence. A few hundred yards further ahead, on your left you will see a low bridge which you drove over to get to the county beach. This is the entrance to Geiger Creek. Pass under the bridge and continue north toward the interior of Boca Chica. Unlike most tidal creeks in the lower

The county beach at Boca Chica Key offers easy access to Geiger Creek.

Keys, this one has little if any actual tidal flow. This is because the creek is interrupted by a paved road that crosses it about a thousand yards upstream where a shallow canal was dredged off to the east. This canal allows water flow from a shallow basin and offers what little tidal effect there is. For this reason, there is considerable buildup of sediment for the first 500 yards from the creek's entrance. Midway, the creek splits, taking on a different look. Where the creek divides, there is a gentle flow that doesn't allow the accumulation of fine sediment. The bottom, therefore, is much harder and, in many places, even sandy. The right fork takes you along a beautiful display of red mangroves that gently touch above your head, forming a splendid canopy. The left fork takes you under the brush for a close view of these magnificent trees. It would be easier to pull yourself along than to even attempt to paddle this portion. The trees are very often so close to the water that only such a vessel as the kayak could even venture through the area. This creek, too, is about 500 yards long. The two portions join again just before they are interrupted by the paved road.

Though this trip ends abruptly, you can take the opportunity as you double-back to explore the side of the split you didn't venture down on your trip into the interior. There are still many wonderful things to see as you pass slowly through these narrow passes. Gray (mangrove) snapper are seen almost continuously along the narrow portions of the creeks. Also, just before the creek ends, on the left side, there are some shallow marshy portions where a variety of night herons and other aquatic birds can be easily viewed during most of the winter months. When you again enter the open Atlantic waters, you may want to visit a shallow patch reef less than a thousand yards offshore from the creek in about 10 feet of water. There diving can easily be done from your kayak.

Geiger Key
(Including Saddlehill Key, Bird Key, and Pelican Key)

While in the neighborhood, you may wish to check out another area that is no stranger to kayakers. Just about a mile or more up Old Boca Chica Road from the county beach, you will find Geiger Road and Geiger Key Marina. Just past the marina, on the left, just before Geiger Road ends, there is an area protected from winds and tides where kayaks can be easily launched. This property is used by private citizens to **launch (7-B)** boats free of charge, and kayakers enjoy the same privilege. This area offers probably the most protected course in the lower Keys when there is a brisk north wind. However, this course is not ideal for a south wind. These islands also have deep water access for powerboats, and caution should always be taken when in these channels. Powerboats can approach from the Saddlebunch Harbor side, as well as the west side of Saddlehill Key, approaching Geiger Key Marina from the south. I have also watched boats pass between Saddlehill Key and Bird Key.

The layout for this course is very simple. Starting from Geiger Key Marina, travel south toward the west end of Saddlehill Key. There you will find a narrow tidal creek that takes a side trip into the interior of the island, displaying some beautiful formations of not only red mangrove, but also black and white mangroves. You should travel east toward Bird Key, staying as close as possible to the coast of Saddlehill Key during windy days. Soon, Bird Key will come into view, and there you have the opportunity to cross over and explore the small island. Along the northwest side of Bird Key, you will again find a narrow tidal creek. You should stay to the northwest side of the island if there is any unfavorable wind. There is a shallow bar that joins the islands of Pelican Key and Saddlehill Key. The bar could very well be the best place for viewing aquatic birds in this area. This particular

A calm, protected put-in, like this one at Geiger Key,
is always a welcome start.

spot could also offer the most difficulty crossing at low tide.
If instead you circle around the south side of Pelican Key, you
may find the going easier. With a brisk north or east wind, you
can enjoy a casual ride back toward the west end of Saddlehill
Key, and from there, a simple crossing to Geiger Key Marina.

Because of the mostly open nature of this area, it can be
used during the summer months as well as the winter
months.

Section III

Advanced Trips

Introduction

 This section offers much longer trips than the ones in the previous section. Some of these trips can cover more than 20 miles. They should be done only under the best conditions and by people who are more experienced with long trips. You may wish to use a rental boat or provide your own boat to ferry your kayaks into these remote areas for exploration. There are also charters that specialize in this sort of trip, so you can let someone else do the planning and preparation and just enjoy the beauty. These offshore islands are worthy of the effort that it takes to venture to them. As mentioned in the first section of this book, there is no camping allowed in these areas.

Two notes of caution: Because of the vastness and remoteness of this area, you should tell someone who'll be staying behind of your trip plans, including your estimated time of return, before heading out. Also, if you choose to ferry your kayak to these areas in a powerboat, be aware that these waters are extremely shallow. Navigating these waters can be a nightmare for the novice mariner. Instructions for navigating a power vessel through these waterways are beyond the scope of this book. Each chapter gives information on the closest marina where a powerboat may be rented. Consult the marina staff for information on navigation to your intended destination.

Islands covered in this section will be those islands that lie north of the main islands of the lower Keys, mostly within the Great White Heron Wildlife Refuge. These islands include Content Keys, Sawyer Key, Johnston Key, Barracuda Keys, Marvin Keys, Snipe Keys, Mud Keys and Lower Harbor Keys. Because of the delicate nature of the refuge, certain restrictions apply in certain areas. These restrictions are outlined in each chapter. As in the previous sections, we will start with those islands most northerly and move south. I have again included charts for your reference. These charts should be used only to familiarize yourself with the area, not for navigation.

8. The Content Keys

*U*se the **launch 3-B,** described on page xx, as a put-in for access to the Content Keys. Before heading out, be sure that you have taken into consideration the winds and tides.

Upon launching your kayak, you should work your way along the coast of Big Torch Key toward the north and cross the small opening that separates Water Keys and Big Torch Key. From the narrows between Water Keys and Big Torch Key, you should see the Content Keys about 3 miles to the north. Huge shoals surround these islands. If you "hop" from Water Keys to the next small island, continuing north toward Content Keys, you should have little problem crossing these flats, unless there is an unusually low tide.

In the winter months you will probably find it easier to keep on the west side of the Water Keys, providing a lee from the winds that prevail at that time of year. The west side can be very shallow at low tide, and it is very rocky. You may need to keep away from the coast.

There are two distinct groups of islands that make up the Content Keys, with an access channel between the two groups. Directly north of the small island past the Water Keys is a grassy shoal with a few small islands in its nucleus. This is the eastern group of the Content Keys These islands are ringed with deeper water all around, which offers a spectacular view of marine animals which, of course, attract aquatic birds of all kinds.

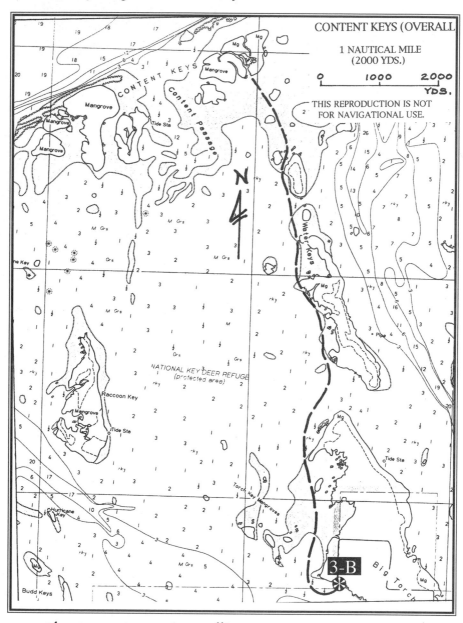

The Content Keys (Overall)

Various species of shorebirds can be found feeding at low tide in the Florida Keys.

The largest of this group, and the farthest out, has tidal creeks that divide the island into three parts. The narrow passages that form the tidal creeks cause tidal waters to flow at an accelerated pace. The bottom is very shallow and mostly a sand/mud mix, almost like clay. It is mostly covered in grasses. This is an excellent area for viewing rays and sharks, as well as other species of fish that live in shallow waters. These narrow passages can offer hours of fun and plenty of opportunities for viewing mangrove formations, a splendor that is repeated time and time again in the Great White Heron National Wildlife Refuge.

From this group of islands, you look across to the west and see the other group of islands that make up the Content Keys. Between these groups of mangrove islands is a shallow trough of current, known as Content Passage. At times the current that divides these island groups can be almost overwhelming. Be careful on a falling tide that you do not get

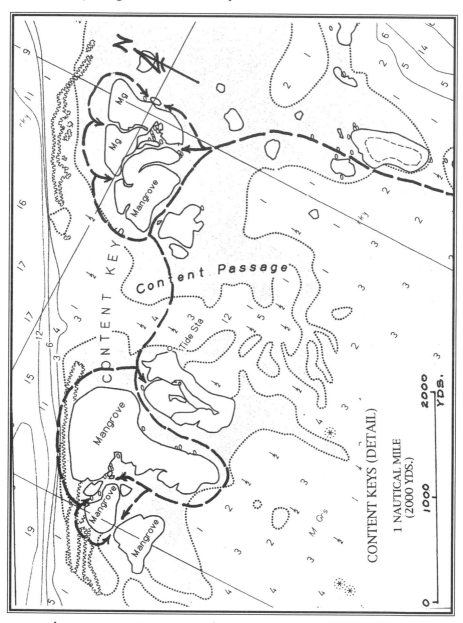

The Content Keys (Detail)

swept out into the Gulf. On your crossing, you will certainly encounter beautiful sandy shoals, where sharks and rays are easy to find.

The western Content Keys form the larger of the groups and have much to offer in the way of exploration. There is a wide, shallow passage that runs between the two main islands of this group, and there are several tidal creeks to explore. The middle of the passage between the two main islands is very sandy. Powerboats are restricted to idle speed in the western Content Keys. However, during low tide, many of these areas are not accessible, even by kayak. Deeper waters are often found closer to the islands where the tides form deep, narrow channels, almost like moats, ringing these tiny islands.

As you return, make sure you head in the proper direction. From here the islands can all look the same. It helps to use a compass heading, and follow its reciprocal upon return. Also, there are always some noticeable landmarks, channel markers, or distinguishable trees. Make a mental note of any of these and anticipate seeing them again upon your return. If you return via a course different from the one you took heading out, be sure that you have ample time to return before dark. This will keep surprises to a minimum and fun to a maximum.

If you choose to **access this area by boat**, you can rent one from any of several marinas in the Big Pine Key area. Boating to the Content Keys will cut down on travel time, increasing your kayaking time in the Content area. The most convenient **rental** spot would be the Old Wooden Bridge Fishing Camp, located at Old Wooden Bridge on Wilder Road on Big Pine Key. See page 87 for directions. This is closest place from which to approach and the deepest channel for navigating the tricky backcountry waters. Consult with marina staff and use a navigational chart of the area to find your way around Harbor Key Bank. Travel west toward the Content Keys from the Gulf side. Anchoring near the most westerly island,

Sea Kayaking in the Florida Keys

Kayaks make it possible to explcre the remote islands of the
Florida Keys without causing destruction to
fragile habitats.

you will find an adequate **put-in site**. Be sure that your anchor
is secure and there is plenty of water so that when you return
in a few hours, your vessel is not aground. Consult the tide
adjustment time on page 9. If there is a brisk north wind, this
trip could be very dangerous and should be postponed until
winds and seas subside.

9. Sawyer Key

(Including Riding Key)

This trip is by far the most challenging of all the advanced trips covered in this section. That is due largely to the fact that there is much open water to cross once you are underway. There is also a deep channel that has considerable tide flow within it. There is, however, an area about halfway where you can pause and stretch. This course is a round trip of approximately 12 nautical miles (or 13.2 statute miles).

The nearest available **launch site** for this trip is **5-A**, the same launch used to access the island of Knockemdown Key, as well as the north end of Cudjoe Key and Little Swash Key. (See page 105 for directions.) Now it serves as the starting point for a much more difficult venture. Standing on this site, you can look north toward the open Gulf and see several small islands off toward the open water and adjacent to Kemp Channel. The nearest island, Budd Key, is just about a mile away. (Budd Key is shown on the Cudjoe Key map on page 104, not the Sawyer Key map.) Beyond it and to the left is another island which seems to have a sandy coastline. This is Tarpon Belly Key. Still further out, near the horizon and a little further left, one island has what looks like a roof structure on one end. Make no mistake, there is a structure in the far northwest end of this island, making this Sawyer Key more easily distinguishable from other islands in that direction.

After making careful plans and checking the weather fore-

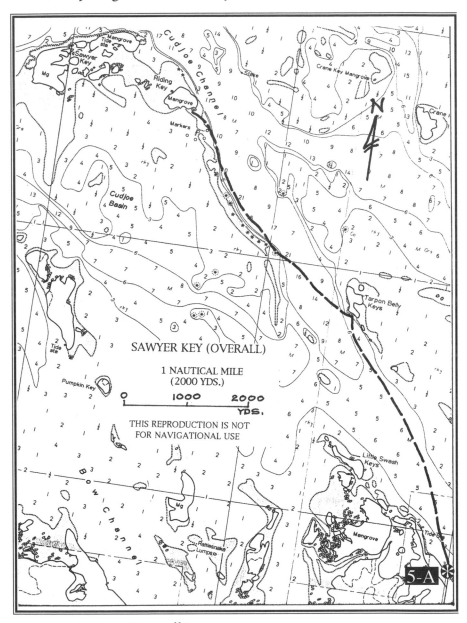

SAWYER KEY (OVERALL)

1 NAUTICAL MILE
(2000 YDS.)

0   1000   2000
YDS.

THIS REPRODUCTION IS NOT
FOR NAVIGATIONAL USE

5-A *

Sawyer Key (Overall)

cast for the day, you can make a heading almost due north from the launch site and cross Kemp Channel toward Budd Key. You should cross on the west side of Budd Key and continue along Kemp Channel to Tarpon Belly Key.

Tarpon Belly Key is a little less than halfway to Sawyer Key. Here, tend to any problems that may have occurred thus far and take a short break. After departing Tarpon Belly, there is no place to stop for 2 nautical miles. Between Tarpon Belly Key and Riding Key, which is at the far south end of Sawyer Key and the nearest landfall from Tarpon Belly, Cudjoe Channel can offer either assistance or hindrance. Shortly after departing Tarpon Belly Key, determine whether the tide is running with or against you. If the tide is running in your favor, continue along the edge of the channel, using the current to assist you. When doing this, keep in mind that powerboaters frequent this channel and, though it is wide, they may not see you until the last minute. If the tide is running against you, cross this channel first and proceed along the shallow waters on the west side toward Riding Key. By avoiding the opposing tide waters, you can make much better time. Use this same rule when returning to the launch.

Riding Key

Upon arriving at Riding Key, you should take a brief, but well deserved, break. The northwest end of Sawyer Key is still over a mile away. The waters between Sawyer Key and Riding Key are very shallow and much easier to endure.

On the south side of Riding Key, especially in the fall and winter months, there are often flocks of various aquatic birds. Though the water on the south end of the island is relatively deep, the north side is considerably shallower and this is where you should pause for a few moments of rest and a good stretch. Looking northwest from here, you can see the main body of Sawyer Key, as well as the protected tidal basin

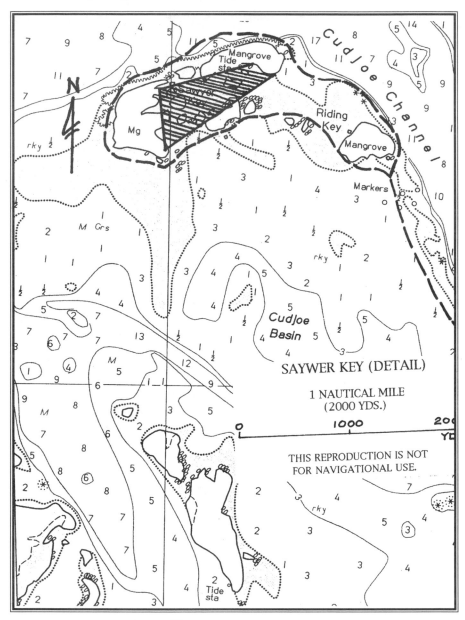

Sawyer Key (Detail)

opposing the open Gulf of Mexico. Though this tidal basin is largely a muddy bottom, there are areas that are sandy and rocky. These rocky areas deserve caution, especially at low tide, because the rocks are very sharp and could damage a kayak.

For those of you who have chosen a powerboat as a means of transporting your kayak, with the intention of kayaking after arrival, the best spot to launch is the south side of Riding Key because the waters there give the boat the best tide adjustment. Cudjoe Key Marina, located at the end of Drost Drive, is the closest marina to the Sawyer Key area (305-745-2357). See page 114 for directions. You can kayak from here all the way around Sawyer Key and back, without concerning yourself whether there will be sufficient water for the boat upon return. Cudjoe Channel is also deep and easily navigated.

Sawyer Key

On a heading that would take you northwest from Riding Key, you start across a shallow tidal basin that supports a wide range of fish and fowl. Fish and Wildlife officials have limited access to a portion of this basin to preserve this fragile habitat. You should act responsibly and stay out of the areas clearly indicated by buoys that state "Vessel Exclusion." There are two areas that are outlined by these buoys; both are on the extreme northern end of the basin, and prohibit access to two narrow tidal creeks in that area. Outside these two areas, there are no other restrictions.

The northwest corner of Sawyer Key is made up of shallow bays and small mangrove islands, rather than of tidal creeks as seen in other islands bordering the Gulf of Mexico. These shallow bays give the aquatic birds wonderful areas in which to sit quietly between feedings. They also provide shelter from winds. Pelicans and frigate birds are found frequently during the winter months. The northwest side has a large sandy bar that extends south and west. Long-legged aquatics stand and feed in shallow tide streams at low tide. Osprey, pelicans, frigate birds, and several other species search the waters below for small weary fish, often distracted by water-borne predators such as barracudas, tarpon, and gray snapper, just to name a few.

Continuing north around to the Gulf side of the island, the bottom nearshore is again shallow and rocky. Be careful of the rocks. On the north side you will find two docks that have long been in need of repair. Here also you will find a natural coastline with several species of coastal vegetation growing right out to the water's edge. The dock farthest east leads out to a ramshackle house. This is the roof that you saw from a distance when heading out. Please respect this property, as well as the vessel exclusion areas.

The sea kayaking enthusiast will find this trip more exciting than others because there is plenty of open water, with little shelter from the elements. A late afternoon return by kayak can give you a sense of peace and serenity since this area is not often traveled. As the sun sets, aquatic birds of this region return to their rookeries. A late day return is easily accomplished because there are only a few islands to interrupt your line of sight between Sawyer and Cudjoe Keys.

A pelican glides over Kemp Channel, near Tarpon Belly Key.

10. The Barracuda Keys

(Including Marvin Key)

S tretching west from Sawyer Key at a distance of about 3 miles are the Barracuda Keys and Marvin Key. Like all the islands that border the Gulf of Mexico, the north side of these islands can be very difficult to access at certain times and under certain weather conditions. These islands, though small, are certainly significant. They have very shallow, grassy flats with numerous tidal troughs feeding from the north into Turkey Basin to the south. At times, when there are extreme low tides, associated lunar effects, and strong winds during the midwinter months, these flats can be completely exposed, making east-to-west passage between these islands and access to the Gulf of Mexico impossible. Upon these tidal flats can be found many of the aquatic birds that give the backcountry its most predominant feature. These flats are also home to brown rays, nurse sharks, lemon sharks, and sport fish such as permit, tarpon, and bonefish. Many types of invertebrates are found across the sandy bottoms that appear periodically among the grassy flats.

Marvin Key

Marvin Key, like any of the areas in this section, requires attention before you head out. A study of the tides as well as special consideration for the next day's weather should be reviewed the night before. The nearest **launch** site is **6-E**, at Sugarloaf Key Marina. You can also use **launch 6-F** at the

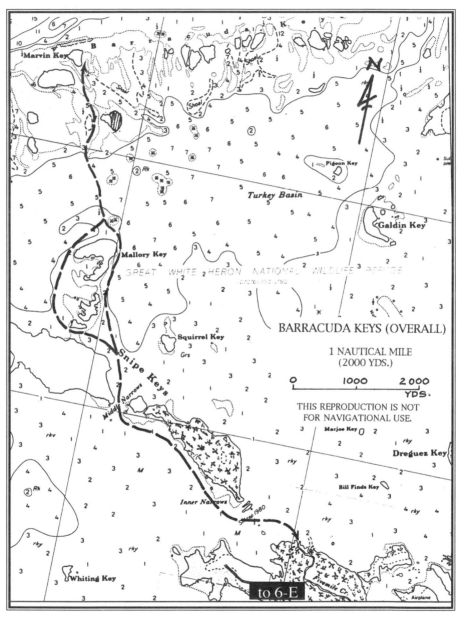

The Barracuda Keys (Overall)

Harris Channel Bridge. See pages 117 and 120 for directions. From the launch, it is 6.5 miles north to Marvin Key. You must cross Turkey Basin to reach Marvin Key. There is little protection from north and east winds on this open water. Of all the trips in this section, this trip could offer the kayaker the most challenge. Accessing this area by powerboat is also very difficult, and I would advise against it unless you have prior knowledge of these waters. The trips immediately following this chapter (Snipe Keys and Mud Keys) offer not only better protection from the winds, as well as other elements, but are about 4 miles closer to the nearest U.S. 1 put-in. If you venture out without the support of a power vessel, you should use Perky and Five-mile Creeks and the islands of Snipe Keys and Mallory Key to protect you from winds and to keep you on course in this unfamiliar area.

After you find your way through Perky Creek or Five-mile Creek, you should cross the Inner Narrows, then follow along the east side of the Snipe Keys. Cross to the Middle Narrows and along the east side of the Snipe Keys to where Mallory Key points north toward Marvin Key. Between Mallory Key and Marvin Key, there is a small island that has no other reference than the fact that the shoal on the east side has been designated a "No Entry" area for the sake of nesting birds. Please respect this area and stay clear.

Low tide can make crossing over to the Gulf from Turkey Basin almost impossible because of numerous shoals. It is best to start from Marvin Key, the northwesternmost island. Marvin Key has a wonderful sandy shoal along its eastern shore and a channel marked out by stakes from Lower Sugarloaf Key (Perky) out to this remote beach site. The channel accommodates shallow draft powerboats. This area is very popular with weekend party-goers since it offers a remote location for sunning and swimming.

If you arrived by boat, anchor your vessel on the south side of this island, then use the beach for your base. Keep in mind that this beach is nearly nonexistent during high tide. Be sure that you leave plenty of water under your boat before heading out. After everything is secure and you are ready to start out, you should concentrate your attention on the islands that lie to the east. These are the Barracuda Keys and the first of them is a mile away.

Barracuda Keys

The Barracuda Keys are small mangrove islands scattered over a mile and half from west to east. These islands can further be divided into three groups, with about a half-mile between each of the groups. Shallow grassy flats buffer all of these islands, but deeper waters are found in narrow tide channels up through the islands running north and south. For this reason, there are times at low tide when it is impossible to cross from east to west and vice versa from one group to the other. At low tide you will have to cross from one group to the other by going south, along the edge of Turkey Basin, and then heading north into the next group. At high tide, however, you can cross from one group into the next one directly. If there is a northeasterly or easterly wind, you may find it easier to start from the furthest islands and work back.

The Barracuda Keys offer a unique look into a vast tide affected area. In its deep and narrow tidal creeks, schools of gray snapper huddle close to the roots of the red mangrove, peeking out only for a glance as you pass by. Small barracudas seeking out an unsuspecting silverside or other small bait fish can be found accompanying these snapper. The hard bottom areas along the tidal creeks support a wide variety of marine sponges as well as other marine invertebrates. Coarse sand, often the skeletal remains of a marine plant called the cactus algae, is found in sloping drifts where the swift current has pushed it up along the sides of faster moving island creeks.

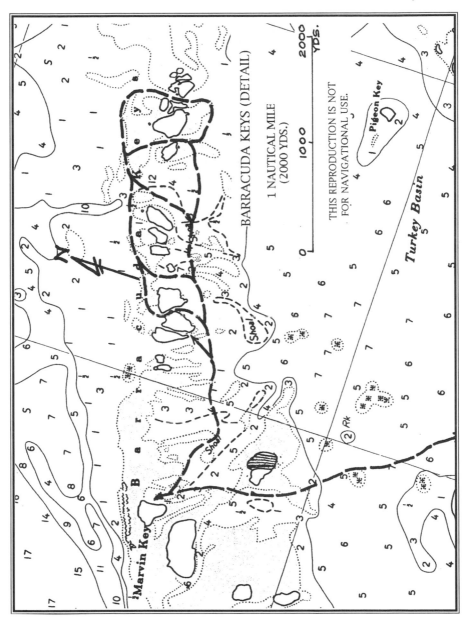

The Barracuda Keys (Detail)

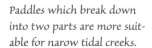

Paddles which break down into two parts are more suitable for narow tidal creeks.

Above the tide, the struggle for aquatic supremacy goes on all along the tidal areas. In the air, pelicans, frigates, royal terns, and osprey take to the air in the search for their daily feed. All across these vast flats the long-legged aquatics — egrets, herons, and ibis — stand on shallow banks or in neighboring tidal pools and streams, patiently waiting for the food that they desperately need to sustain another day. Double-crested cormorant, diving repeatedly in search of food, complete this drama that unfolds daily in many areas throughout the lower Florida Keys, but none quite as noticeably as here in the Barracuda Keys.

You should start out on this trip very early in the morning. Pace yourself throughout the day, and return while there is still plenty of daylight. Rest well before returning to ensure that you have the energy to navigate the critical crossover areas such as the Middle and Inner Narrows, and to find Five-mile or Perky Creek. You will need plenty of daylight to help you through these areas. The distance from either Sugarloaf Key Marina or Harris Channel Bridge to Marvin Key is 12 nautical miles (13.2 statute miles) round trip. Traveling from the put-in at Harris Channel Bridge through Five-mile Creek makes the trip about a mile shorter overall.

11. The Snipe Keys

The Snipe Keys are a kayaker's paradise. They are the most exciting, as well as the most remote, anywhere in the Florida Keys. Nowhere else is such a diversity of marine life and bottom contrasts found. Located in the heart of the Great White Heron Wildlife Refuge and at the southern edge of the Gulf of Mexico, the Snipe Keys display a wonderful array of not only birds but also fish and even coral. They are the most stunning backdrop for kayaking anywhere. The scene is completed with a white sand beach in the northernmost point. The most fascinating features of this island group for kayakers are the tidal creek areas that dissect the northernmost island. It is here that kayaking in the Keys takes on new meaning.

The charts provided in this section reveal that the northern end of the Snipe Keys, the side closest to the Gulf of Mexico, is divided into three sections: east, middle, and west. All three sections are accessible by kayak, without restrictions. The eastern and middle sections, which include the sandy point on the north end, can be explored relatively easily. The west end of the Snipe Keys is a tangled web of narrow streams between mangrove roots that often impede progress and can even cause injury if you're not careful. Extreme caution should be used here, especially during the spring tide effects. (See pages 8–12 for a discussion of tides and weather.) There is little, if anything, to help you find your way along these

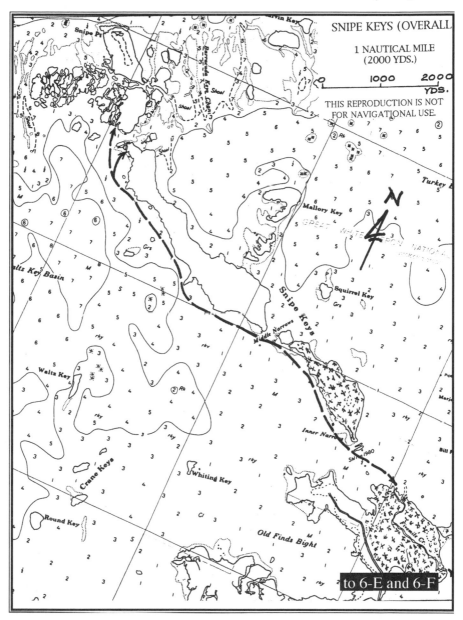

The Snipe Keys (Overall)

western tidal creeks, other than your own sense of direction. Because the islands are small, you will either spill out into the Gulf or on the shore side of the islands.

Whether you choose the less challenging courses to the east, or set the pace for adventure and travel west, the sights and sounds that surround you will take you to a time long forgotten, even in this part of the world. The Snipe Keys have the most to offer everyone by far. There are shallow patch reefs, excellent for snorkeling, off the northern end. You can also try snorkeling in the creeks, using extreme caution with the tide. It is best to use a line from your kayak and keep it with you as you drift along. Whether you choose reef or creek, you will find an array of marine life. One could spend days just exploring this vast area of tidal feed waters.

The Snipe Keys lie some 8 miles north of the Saddlebunch Keys. There are two points of access. You can use **launch 6-E** at Sugarloaf Key Marina (see page 117 for directions) and paddle through Perky Creek (see page 119 for details) and follow the Snipe Keys northwest toward Snipe Point. This passage is nearly 8 miles with one large body of open water to cross between Perky Creek and the Inner Narrows. By following the Snipe Keys on the west side, you will be best protected by the effects of wind.

An easier and shorter route can be made by using **launch 6-F**, just south of Sugarloaf Key near Five-mile Creek. (See page 120 for directions.) From this launch you will have little open water to cross and can explore Five-mile Creek on your way, as well a save about a mile in travel distance to Snipe Key.

Whether you depart from Lower Sugarloaf Key or Harris Channel, a long day is ahead. Be sure to bring plenty of water, food, and current charts of the area. Thoroughly check the weather for the immediate future.

For those of you who wish to explore this wonderful area by kayak but don't want to work for hours to get there, **rental**

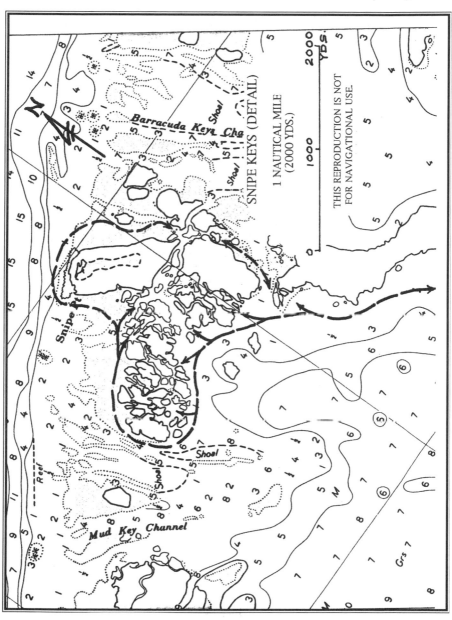

The Snipe Keys (Detail)

Snipe Point, located on the north end of the Snipe Keys, offers a stunning view of tidal flats and sandbars during low tide.

boats are available at several marinas in the Key West area. The safest passage is to go around to the Gulf side of Key West, then travel northeast toward the Snipe Keys along the southern edge of the Gulf of Mexico. Marina staff can assist you further in planning your course. Travel time from Key West by powerboat is about 30 minutes. You can anchor safely on Snipe Point. Be sure your vessel has enough water under it to allow for tide adjustment. For information on tides relative to Snipe Key, see page 9.

North of the Outer Narrows is a cluster of islands that make up a unique and challenging place for the kayaker. It is here that even the skill of white water kayaking can be of some use, for the tides in certain areas run swift enough to be considered dangerous, and low tree branches can complicate matters even more. Whether the tide is coming in or going out, the narrow passages that make for the most challenging aspect of the trip are often no wider than the kayak itself. Add to that the tide forcing its way through the narrow pass and you could find yourself in fast-moving water with no control. There are numerous tidal passes that are totally overgrown, forcing the water under the mangroves and leaving the kayak no place to go. I have explored this area extensively over the years and have taken thousands of novice and first-time kayakers through this area. Before a trip to the Snipe Keys, you may want to brush up on the kayaking techniques discussed in Chapter 1. Here's a quick review; you may want to refer to page 4 for more information.

- Always work against the tide in narrow tidal streams.
- When working with more than one kayak, allow thirty feet or more between boats.
- Use a paddle that can be broken down into two parts, using one half of it like a conventional canoe paddle in tight areas.
- Approach unfamiliar turns slowly.
- If working downstream, let the speed of the water move you along while you use the paddle to steer and to repel trees.

Continuing northward from the Outer Narrows, you start to cross narrow tide streams that shortly thereafter become the main channel of Snipe Key. This main channel divides Snipe Key. There are several markers in the axis of this channel. Each indicates the type of activity allowed in each area. To the west, the marker indicates "No Internal Combustion Engines" and to the east, "No Wake." None of these restrictions apply to the kayaker. In fact, these restrictions will make your experience more pleasant.

The west end of Snipe Key holds the most fascination. Toward Mud Key Channel, the waters are often the clearest of all the Keys backcountry. Here the tide waters of the Gulf of Mexico force themselves through the labyrinth of mangroves toward Waltz Key Basin. Later, they rush back out with the same force to return to the Gulf. In areas where the tide moves with the most force, the bottom is free of sediment and sand, providing a good habitat for marine sponges. Along the edges of the mangrove, steep banks are formed. In places the tide water does not affect, you'll find an accumulation of sand. The sand bottom is home to starfish, sea cucumbers, and mollusks. It is not uncommon to encounter large stingrays and sharks on these sandy bars. At extreme low tides, these bars may require short portages. It is possible travel across the west end of the Snipe Keys using only the tide to propel you, but you might not be able to do it on your first try.

If you travel north through the main channel, you will at last find the Gulf of Mexico. Here you can rest and stretch your legs and become more familiar with the surroundings. There are sandbars on all sides of this point and only the west side has this deep channel. You can travel along the edge of the deep channel that skirts the sandbar. You'll see that on one side of your kayak there will be very little water, and on

A sandbar at the Snipe Keys offers a moment to park and enjoy the beauty of the Florida Keys.

the other it will be too deep to see bottom.

If you kayak east from the main channel, you'll find deeper waters that flow more gently. In some places the water will be more than 25 feet deep. About 400 yards east of the main channel, you once again come to an intersection. You can continue east, but there is more to explore if you turn north toward Snipe Point. On the east side of the point are some of the most beautiful sandbars, which at low tide become beaches. During extreme low tides the beach can run the entire distance between Snipe Key and Marvin Key and beyond. Aquatic birds feed in this area at low tide; just about every species of nearshore fish found in the Keys feeds here at high tide.

When you're ready to begin your return, head through the southeast portion of the Snipe Keys, through tidal passages similar to the western portion, minus the raging currents. These passages terminate at the Outer Narrows, and from there you can start on your way back. You're sure to feel tired after a full day of adventure in the Snipe Keys, but you'll want to make the 20-mile round trip again, to explore more of these seemingly endless tidal creeks.

12. The Mud Keys

A s are most of the islands in this section, this island group is not only remote, but unique. Unlike the rugged and challenging Snipe Keys, this set of islands is very tranquil and easy to explore.

To travel by boat to the Mud Keys, you'll want to rent a boat from a marina in Key West, as you would to reach the Snipe Keys. See page 160 for more information. The Mud Keys are about 2 miles closer than the Snipe Keys. Ferrying your kayak is a good option for windier days when crossing the open water could be physically demanding.

The nearest starting point to the Mud Keys for a kayak launch is Big Coppitt Key. From here you can **launch (12-A)** from a remote site on the north end of the island. Traveling south along U.S. 1, pass mile marker 10. Immediately on the right-hand side is a restaurant called Bobalu's. Turning here you will be on Fourth Street. Drive along until it comes to F Avenue, then turn left. Travel F Avenue until you come to Barcelona Drive, where you turn right. Where Barcelona Drive ends, you will find a small public access boat ramp. Launching from here, you are about 4 nautical miles (4.4 statute miles) from the Mud Keys. There is mostly open water between the launch and the Mud Keys. Travel northwest, toward Duck Key, then continue on toward Fish Hawk Key. From Fish Hawk, travel north to the Mud Keys. Be careful on windy days.

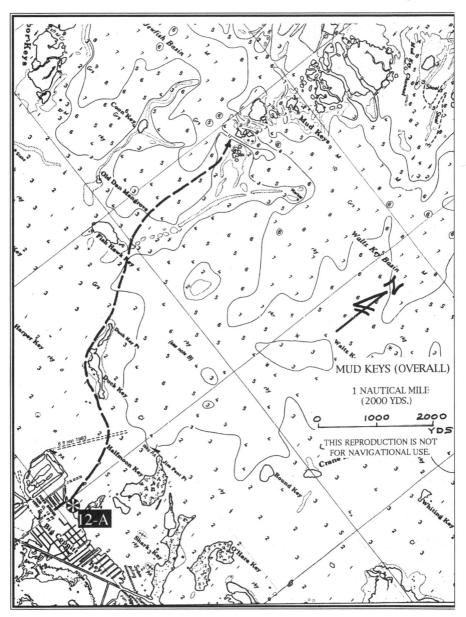

The Mud Keys (Overall)

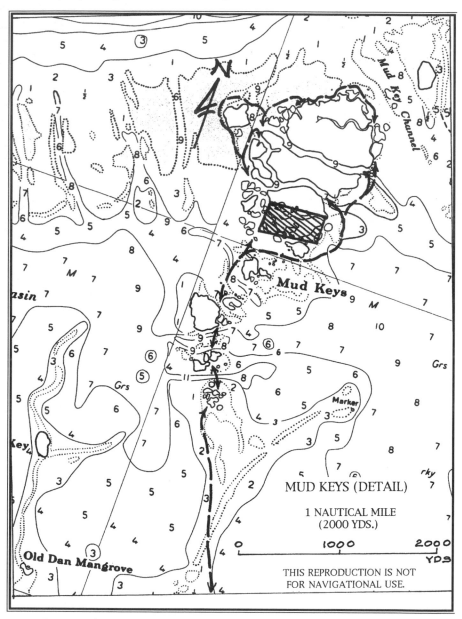

The Mud Keys (Detail)

The Mud Keys can be thought of as one island divided by at least three deep channels, with a grouping of smaller mangroves on the south end. These deeper channels run nearly east-west through the hub of the main island. Tide affects these creeks from both directions through these main arteries. Tides usually run from west to east on the incoming tide and east to west on the outgoing tide. Because these channels are deep and wide, they run more slowly and smoothly that those at Snipe Keys.

Whether you arrive by powerboat or by paddling your kayak, starting from the west side of the island is best. In the far northwest corner of the Mud Keys lies a small island with a small sandy landing that is ideal for regrouping and resting after a long paddle. This spot is also the hub of all the main channels that affect the Mud Keys. This spot is easily found and should be used anytime you need rest or reassurance of your location.

From this vantage point, the tide either flows from the north out of the Gulf on the incoming tide or flows past here going north on the outgoing tide. For the tide adjustments between West Harbor Key and Snipe Key, see page 9 in the section on tide and weather.

Two areas of interest are found in the Mud Keys. First is the area directly bordering the Gulf of Mexico on the north side of the island. Some of the oldest mangrove development is found overgrowing narrow tidal creeks that flow into beautiful coves. The shallow, grassy flats between the north side and the Gulf of Mexico are often teeming with invertebrates and small shark and rays, especially at or near the low tides.

The other area of interest is down the west side of the main islands, going south from your starting point and continuing through the narrow, shallow portions of the southern end of the island. There are several narrow, but firm, sandbars that are very friendly for exploring. Often the tide rushes over these shallow strips, making them very inviting. Also, toward the interior of the island is an area that nesting birds call home in the winter. For this reason, this area is a "vessel exclusion area" and all entry is prohibited. Buoys that clearly mark this area. Please respect these closed areas and stay clear of them.

The Mud Keys are fascinating, beautiful, and too vast for complete description. They are unique in their wonderful mix of wide, deep channels and their shallow, vibrant shoals and sandbars. I have attempted to help the first-time visitor find and see what is available in this unique marine setting.

As you make your return late in the day, you will find the islands of Fish Hawk and Duck Key alive with aquatic birds coming in for the evening. At Fish Hawk Key during the winter and spring, majestic frigate birds can be seen by the hundreds in the early evening. This trip by kayak is about 15 miles overall.

Mangrove canopies, resembling tunnels, allow kayakers a privileged view of the mystic nature of the Mud Keys.

Wide boulevards of deep tidal water are also found at the Mud Keys.

13. The Lower Harbor Keys

(Including Channel Key and Cayo Agua)

This chapter covers the southernmost islands of the lower Keys, the Lower Harbor Keys. These islands are 4 nautical miles (4.4 statute miles) north of Stock Island. As with many of the trips in the Advanced Section, there is much open water between the launch and the islands. Study weather and tides before heading out.

You can easily access this area by parking along the shoulder of U.S. 1, just after the Boca Chica Bridge (mile marker 6). **Launch (13-A)** on the north side. (Accessing this area by powerboat is not recommended.) From here you can look north toward these islands, just beyond the power lines offshore. The first island is Channel Key. This small island is surrounded by shoals with a deep moatlike channel dividing it in half. Here you can explore the mangrove canopies with their soft cool lighting and gray snapper hiding among the prop roots.

After stopping for a brief visit, continue north toward Cayo Agua. Along the way, you could even explore Grassy Key, though there is little of any significance there. Cayo Agua, however, offers a wonderful view of red mangrove under extreme tidal effect. Caution should be used when exploring here. Like Channel Key, Cayo Agua is divided by a tidal creek down the middle, and is ringed with deeper water. These creeks can run very swiftly, creating tricky situations during

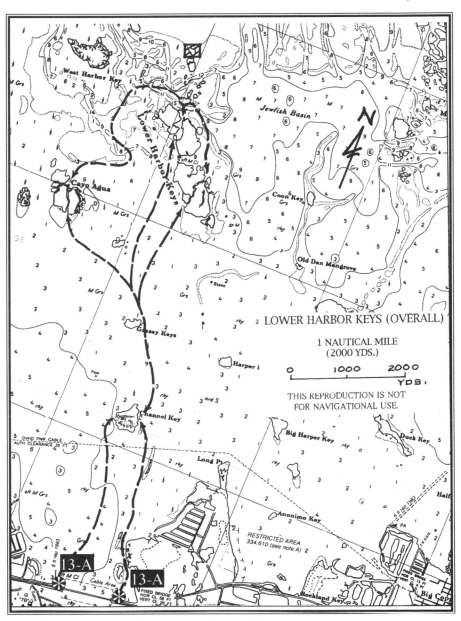

The Lower Harbor Keys (Overall)

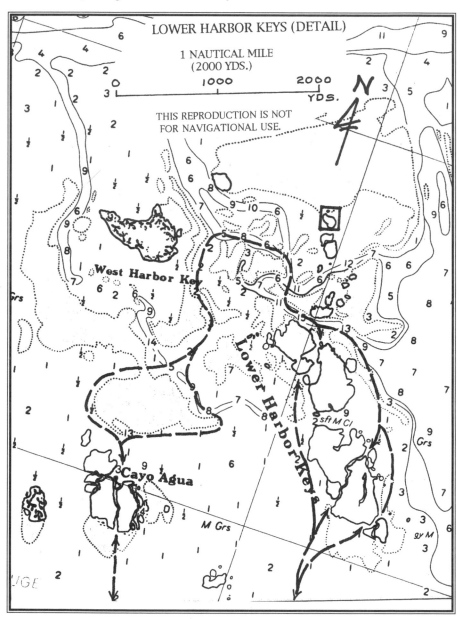

The Lower Harbor Keys (Detail)

extreme tides. If you wish to go no further north, you will have certainly seen the best part of this area.

If you wish to explore further and see the Lower Harbor Keys, then you should head in a northeasterly direction, crossing several areas of deep, tidal water. If you start at the top of the Lower Harbor Keys and work south, you can criss-cross narrow tidal creeks on your way home. These enormous tidal flats can be an exceptional area for viewing aquatic birds. There is also a good chance of seeing small sharks and rays. On extreme low tides, you may have difficulty crossing some areas. The deeper channel on the east side of the Lower Harbor Keys spills out of Jewfish Basin and into the Gulf of Mexico and can have extreme tidal flow.

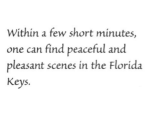

Within a few short minutes, one can find peaceful and pleasant scenes in the Florida Keys.

Bibliography

Coffey, D. J. *Dolphins, Whales & Porpoises, An Encyclopedia of Sea Mammals.* New York: Macmillan Publishing Co., Inc., 1977.

Dance, S. Peter. *Shells.* New York: Dorling Kindersley, Inc., 1992.

Gluckman, David. *Sea Kayaking in the Florida Keys.* Sarasota: Pineapple Press, Inc., 1995.

Hardin, E. Dennis. "Dry, sunny pinelands unlike cool, shady hammocks." *The Key West Citizen,* (date not available) 1995.

Henry, James A. et.al. *The Climate and Weather of Florida.* Sarasota: Pineapple Press, 1994.

Hiaasen, Scott. "State officials nearing agreement on lobster season." *The Miami Herald,* (date not available) 1994. p. 1, col. 1-3.

Hoffmeister, J. G. *Land From the Sea.* Miami, Florida: University Miami Press, 1974.

Humann, Paul. *Reef Creature Identification, Florida, Caribbean, Bahama.* Jacksonville, Florida: New World Press, 1989.

Kale, H. W. & Maehr, D. S. *Florida's Birds.* Sarasota, Florida: Pineapple Press, 1990.

Lais, Sami. "Volunteers Chart Algae Bloom." *Florida Keys Keynoter,* March 26, 1994. p. 1, col. 1-3.

Meinkoth, Norman A. *National Audubon Society, Field Guide to North American Seashore Creatures.* New York: Alfred A. Knopf, 1994.

Mueller, E. et.al. *The Monroe County Environmental Story.* Big Pine Key, Florida: Sea Camp Association Inc., 1991.

Robins, R. C. and Ray, C. G. *A Field Guide To Atlantic Coast Fishes, North America.* Boston: Houghton Mifflin Company, 1986.

Sigo, Kelly. "Conchs get help, not hurt, from man." *Florida Keys Keynoter.* October 28, 1995. p. 1, col 1-5.

Steinman, Jon. "Sponge die-off punctuates bay crisis." *The Key West Citizen,* October 8, 1995. p. 1, col 1-5.

Index

Sea Kayaking in the Florida Keys

Sea Kayaking in the Florida Keys

Here are some other books from Pineapple Press on related topics. For a complete catalog, write to Pineapple Press, P.O. Box 3899, Sarasota, Florida 34230-3899, or call (800) 746-3275.

Sea Kayaking in Florida by David Gluckman. This guide to sea kayaking in Florida for novices and experienced paddlers alike includes information on wildlife, camping, and gear; maps of the Big Bend Sea Grasses Saltwater Paddling Trail; tips on kayaking the Everglades; lists of liveries and outfitters; and more.

Adventure Sports in Florida by Bruce Hunt. More than a guidebook, this lively chronicle of the author's adventures in high-adrenaline sports schools in Florida puts you in the "hot seat" every time.

The Surfer's Guide to Florida by Amy Vansant. The first comprehensive guide to the waves of Florida offers locations, swell conditions, and particulars of nearly 200 of Florida's best surfing destinations, including where to park and how to get to the beach, whom you might meet, and inside information on the local scene.

The *Exploring Wild* series: A series of field guides, each with information on all the parks, preserves, and natural areas in its region, including wildlife to look for and best time of year to visit.
    Exploring Wild Central Florida by Susan D. Jewell. From New Smyrna and Crystal River in the north to Hobe Sound and Punta Gorda in the south, including Lake Okeechobee.
    Exploring Wild North Florida by Gil Nelson. From the Suwannee River to the Atlantic shore, and south to include the Ocala National Forest.
    Exploring Wild Northwest Florida by Gil Nelson. The Florida Panhandle, from the Perdido River in the west to the Suwannee River in the east.
    Exploring Wild South Florida, Second Edition by Susan D. Jewell. From Hobe Sound and Punta Gorda south to include the Keys and the Dry Tortugas. This new expanded edition includes over 40 new natural areas and covers Broward, Hendry, Lee, and Palm Beach Counties as well as Dade, Collier, and Monroe. With this edition the entire state of Florida is covered in the four-volume Exploring Wild Florida set.

Florida's Birds: A Handbook and Reference by Herbert W. Kale II and David S. Maehr. This guide to identification, enjoyment, and protection of Florida's varied and beautiful population of birds identifies and discusses over 325 species, with information on distinguishing marks, habitat, season, and distribution.

The Trees of Florida by Gil Nelson. The first comprehensive guide to Florida's amazing variety of tree species, this book serves as both a reference and a field guide.

The Shrubs and Woody Vines of Florida by Gil Nelson. A companion to *The Trees of Florida*, this reference and field guide covers over 550 species of native and naturalized woody shrubs and vines.

The Everglades: River of Grass, 50th Anniversary Edition by Marjory Stoneman Douglas. This is the treasured classic of nature writing, first published fifty years ago, that captured attention all over the world and launched the fight to save the Everglades. The 50th Anniversary Edition includes an update on the events in the Glades in the last ten years.

Guide to the Lake Okeechobee Area by Bill and Carol Gregware. The first comprehensive guidebook to this area of the state includes a 110-mile hike/bike tour on top of the Herbert Hoover Dike encircling the lake, part of the Florida National Scenic Trail.

Poisonous Plants and Animals of Florida and the Caribbean by David W. Nellis. An illustrated guide to the characteristics, symptoms, and treatments for over 300 species of poisonous plants and toxic animals.

Seashore Plants of South Florida and the Caribbean by David W. Nellis. A full-color guide to the flora of nearshore environments, including complete characteristics of each plant as well as ornamental, medicinal, ecological and other aspects. Suitable for backyard gardeners and serious naturalists.

The Florida Keys: A History of the Pioneers by John Viele. The trials and successes of the Keys pioneers are brought to life in this affectionate and respectful account of the early life of one of Florida's most treasured areas.

Shipwrecks of Florida: A Comprehensive Listing by Steven D. Singer. General information on research, search and salvage, wreck identification, artifact conservation, and rights to wrecks accompanies a listing of 2100 wrecks off the Florida coast from the sixteenth century to the present.

The Climate and Weather of Florida by James A. Henry, Kenneth M. Portier, and Jan Coyne. This comprehensive book offers in-depth, clear explanations of the entire range of Florida's weather.

The Springs of Florida by Doug Stamm. Take a guided tour of Florida's fascinating springs in this beautiful book featuring detailed descriptions, maps, and rare underwater photography. Learn how to enjoy these natural wonders while swimming, diving, canoeing, and tubing.